Chinese Religion and Familism

Also available from Bloomsbury:

Buddhism, Education and Politics in Burma and Thailand,
Khammai Dhammasami
Chinese Religion, Xinzhong Yao
Confucianism in China, Tony Swain
Religion and Orientalism in Asian Studies, edited by Kiri Paramore
Religions of Beijing, edited by You Bin and Timothy Knepper

Chinese Religion and Familism

*The Basis of Chinese Culture,
Society, and Government*

Jordan Paper

BLOOMSBURY ACADEMIC
LONDON • NEW YORK • OXFORD • NEW DELHI • SYDNEY

BLOOMSBURY ACADEMIC
Bloomsbury Publishing Plc
50 Bedford Square, London, WC1B 3DP, UK
1385 Broadway, New York, NY 10018, USA

BLOOMSBURY, BLOOMSBURY ACADEMIC and the Diana logo are trademarks
of Bloomsbury Publishing Plc

First published in Great Britain 2020

Cover design by Maria Rajka
Cover image © Muhammad Raden / PACIFIC PRESS / Alamy Stock Photo.

A catalogue record for this book is available from the British Library.

A catalog record for this book is available from the Library of Congress.

ISBN: HB: 978-1-3501-0361-0
PB: 978-1-3501-0360-3
ePDF: 978-1-3501-0363-4
eBook: 978-1-3501-0362-7

Typeset by Deanta Global Publishing Services, Chennai, India

To find out more about our authors and books visit www.bloomsbury.com
and sign up for our newsletters.

*For the many in Taiwan and Mainland China who facilitated
my research and offered valued friendship over the
last half century.*

Contents

Figures

All images are the author's own.

Frontispiece: Logograph for *xiao* (Familism) in script of time of Kongzi (Confucius) by author.

Acknowledgments

These studies of Chinese Religion are a result of joint research with my life partner, Zhuang Li, who in so many ways enhanced the studies. My work on Chinese Religion began in earnest after our marriage in Taiwan forty-five years ago and has continued there and on the Mainland of China unabated ever since. This book would not have come about if it were not for the Centre for the Study of Religion and Society at the University of Victoria (British Columbia), which for two decades, ever since I retired from York University (Toronto), has provided me with a scholarly home. I especially thank those colleagues at the Centre who read parts of this book and provided important feedback as well as encouragement.

Lucy Carroll, an editor at Bloomsbury Publishing, did magnificent work in shepherding this book through the approval process, and I am most grateful to her for her understanding of a difficult proposal. I thank all the others at Bloomsbury for facilitating the publishing of the work. Daniel Overmyer read the manuscript for the press and pointed out areas that needed further study, thus enhancing the book.

Parts of this book have been presented at conferences and received valuable feedback, and earlier versions of a few parts have been published in various formats:

An early version of Chapter 3 was presented as a plenum address at the Republic of China Centenary International Conference: Religion in Taiwan in 2011 entitled, "The Impact of the West on the Understanding of Chinese Religion." This address was expanded into a series of lectures given at Beijing Normal University in 2012. I am grateful to Yang Lihui, my former student and chair of and professor in the Department of Folkloristics, and An Deming, professor of folklore at the Institute of Literature at the Chinese Academy of Social Sciences, for making these and later similar arrangements. On request of the editors, a version of these lectures was published as "A New Approach to Understanding Chinese Religion" as the first article in the first issue of *Huaren zongjiao yenchio (Studies in Chinese Religion)* 2013.

An early version of Chapter 5 was given at the Religious Thought and Lived Religion in China Conference at the University of British Columbia in 2002. The conference proceedings were published, including my paper "The Role of Possession Trance in Chinese Culture and Religion: A Comparative Overview from the Neolithic to the Present," in Philip Clart & Paul Crow, eds., *The People and The Dao: New Studies in Chinese Religion in Honor of Daniel L. Overmyer*, Monumenta Serica Monograph LX (2009): 327–48.

An early version of Chapter 6 was given as a lecture at Beijing Normal University in 2014 but not previously published.

Chapter 9 reflects the work that led to my *The Theology of the Chinese Jews, 1000–1850* (Waterloo, ON: Wilfrid Laurier University Press, 2012). An early version of the chapter was given as a lecture series at Beijing Normal University in 2012 and published on request as "The Theology of the Chinese Jews: An Understanding of God that is Simultaneously Jewish, 'Confucian' and Daoist," in Jeanine Diller and Asa Kasher, eds., *Models of God and Alternative Ultimate Realities* (Springer, 2013), 497–510.

All photographs are my own and were digitized by myself into black and white renditions from color slides taken from 1965 to virtually the present in Taiwan, Mainland China, and Victoria (British Columbia).

Prologue: Six Decades of Studying Chinese Religion

My previous book on Chinese Religion, *The Spirits are Drunk: Comparative Approaches to Chinese Religion*, was published in 1995, although the manuscript was completed nearly a decade earlier and the research went back to the 1960s. Since that time, the field of the study of Chinese Religion in contrast to religion in China, whose deficiency I had criticized, has expanded enormously and many excellent studies have been written; extensive traveling in China has broadened my perception of the relationship between the state and religion in China; my scholarly interests shifted from comparative religion in general to comparative theology; and I developed an interest in Chinese Judaism. Hence, my previous book, in parts, was out of date and furthermore did not reflect my last thirty years of research on the subject.

The Spirits are Drunk began with an argument for a single Chinese religion based on the study of ritual, and it analyzed the Chinese understanding of the mystic experience as well as its influence on aesthetics. These parts, I believe, still hold and will not be repeated here. Instead, this book focuses on the ideological basis of Chinese Religion and how it fits into religion globally. In doing so, comparative religion will be critiqued as often being an exercise in Christian ethnocentrism, including studies in the new field of cognitive studies of religion. Originally, comparative religion provided an ideological basis for Western colonialism, and today this predilection continues to be seen, albeit more subtly, in some religious studies works. Hence, paradigms for studying religion alternate to that of the Christian paradigm will be presented and explored as a means for understanding Chinese Religion, and those similar to it, as part of a global religious construct I call "Familism."

This book will also explore the theology of Chinese Religion, not in the literal sense of the word, discussed in the book, but more generally, as reflecting how people of a culture understand, both intellectually and emotionally, the nature of existence and the meaning of life and death. The interaction of foreign religions in China—Buddhism, Christianity, and Judaism—will be also explored in these regards. Hopefully, this book will present a more nuanced means for understanding the religion of almost a quarter of the world's population, as well as the indigenous religions of the rest of Asia, sub-Saharan Africa, Polynesia, and other contemporary traditions and the religion of the classic Roman world and early Israelite religion.

Chinese terms are often confusing in a work like this one because there has been a change in the accepted method of Romanization of Chinese logographs. Until the mid-twentieth century, and in some places for a few years afterward, the Wade-Giles system was utilized. But after the end of the civil war, a new system, called Pinyin, was adopted. Slowly but not consistently publications began to use the new Romanization system (and in Taiwan more recently a third system is used). In this work, Pinyin will be used with the Wade-Giles Romanization put into parentheses in cases where readers may be more familiar with the older system—for example, *Tian* (*T'ien*), Dao (Tao). Even older systems are still used for place names in Taiwan—for example, Taipei.

Chinese Religion: The Oldest Documented Religious Tradition

Xiao ("Filial Piety" or "Familism")

From the approximately three-thousand-year-old *Classic of Odes (Shijing)*, we find the following in a ritual ode (#209):

> We plant panicled millet and glutinous millet; our panicled millet is rich, our glutinous millet is growing in orderly rows; our granaries are full, our sheaves in myriads of myriads; and so we make wine and food, we make offerings and sacrifice, we make the incorporator of the dead sit at ease, we encourage him to eat; and so increase our great felicity. Stately are the movements; pure are your oxen and sheep; with them you go and perform the winter sacrifice, the autumn sacrifice . . . the offering ritual is brilliant; the deceased ancestors are exalted; the ancestral spirits enjoy the offering; the pious descendant will enjoy happiness; they [the spirits] will requite him with increased felicity, a longevity of a myriad years without limit . . . The ceremonies are now completed . . . then all the male members of the clan celebrate the feast [eat the food offered to the spirits] . . . the ancestral spirits have enjoyed the wine and food, they will cause the lord to have a long life; you have been very compliant, very correct, doing everything to the utmost; may sons and grandsons without interruption continue it. (Karlgren 1950: 162–63—with minor modifications)

From the over two-thousand-year-old *Classic of Xiao* (Familism), chapter 16, we find the following:

> The Master [Confucius] said: In the past, the brilliant kings served their fathers with filial piety, and thus intelligently served Sky, served their mothers with filial piety, and thus carefully served Earth. . . . Sky and Earth served with intelligence and care, the ancestral spirits brilliantly manifest themselves. . . . [The kings] respectfully made offerings at the ancestral temple, demonstrating their

remembrance of their parents. . . . They respectfully made offerings at the ancestral temple, and the spirits of the dead arrived. When their filial piety and fraternal duties were perfected, it reached the bright [ancestral] spirits and their [virtue] illuminated all within the four seas [the world]; there was nowhere [their power] did not penetrate. (Own translation)

From the nearly-thousand-year-old *Family Rituals* of Zhu Xi, the foremost theorist of the Song dynasty, we find the following:

When a man of virtue builds a house his first task is always to set up an offering hall to the east of the main room of his house. For this hall four altars to hold the spirit tablets of the ancestors are made. . . . Once the hall is completed, early each morning the master enters the outer gate to pay a visit. All comings and goings are reported there. On New Year's Day, the solstices, and each new and full moon, visits are made. On the customary festivals, seasonal foods are offered, and when an event occurs, reports are made[before the spirit tablets]. . . . As one generation succeeds another, the spirit tablets are reinscribed and moved to their new places. (Ebrey 1991: 5)

In contemporary China, presently a highly developed technological society, the above delineated religious modality continues unabated:

Drawing on the first nationwide survey of Chinese citizens' spiritual lives, [it is reported] that 182 million Chinese adults embrace ancestor worship practices and beliefs in Reform Era China. This survey-based evidence echoes the large number of ethnographic studies that show a trend toward revitalization of traditional culture, including ancestor worship. (Hu and Tian 2018: 1)

The Chinese Communist Party at first attempted to destroy the traditional family-oriented religion, hoping to move people's allegiances to Chinese society as a whole, especially during the Cultural Revolution. The result was social chaos and the destruction of morality, as well as common politeness and courtesy. Since then, the Party has slowly reinvigorated this religion, understanding that it is the basis of social order in China. Hence, a major reason for the relatively recent huge development of modern transportation infrastructure in China costing billions of dollars is the need to move hundreds of millions of Chinese twice a year to their home areas for the Spring Festival and Qingming in order to participate in family and clan rituals.

In this book, this religion will be called "Chinese Religion" (*huaranjiao*); that is, the religion of the Chinese, just as Judaism is the religion of the Jews. This religion can be summed up in a single word: *xiao*. The logograph for *xiao* consists of the glyph for an aged person over that for a child. (See frontispiece image of an early form of the logograph going back approximately three thousand years.) The word is commonly translated as "filial piety," which is misleading as "piety" implies a Puritan-like religious consciousness. Rosemont and Ames (2009) translate the word as "family reverence," which is much closer to the Chinese meaning. Here, the word will be translated as "Familism," a religious construct found in a number of cultures around the world, in which the family, in and of itself, is the religious focus. "Familism" will be further introduced and discussed in Chapter 3, and its ideology will be analyzed in Chapter 4.

As can be seen in the above, texts describing this religion can be traced back three thousand years, and relevant written material on oracular material (inscribed on scapula of oxen and plastrons of tortoises) go back another five hundred years. Similar shapes and decor of offering vessels for clan ancestral offering rituals go back well into the neolithic period. Hence, Chinese Religion is at least five thousand years old and probably several thousand years older. Thus, Chinese Religion is the oldest religion in the world continuing into the present for which we have documentary evidence.

Xiao continues to be central to Chinese ideology, as it is presently being promoted as the basis of Chinese culture and socialism: "General Secretary Xi Jinping has emphasized many times . . . *xiao* is the heart of traditional culture . . . [and the] core value of socialism" (*People's Daily* [an organ of the Chinese Communist Party] 2016—trans. from the Chinese by Li Chuang Paper). Reversing earlier attitudes of the Chinese Communist Party, Xi frequently refers to *jia* ("*family*") approvingly, reiterating a popular folk expression: *Jia he wan shi xing* ("If the family is united, then everything flourishes").

Chinese Religion is based on family and clan. In most homes, there is a family altar, enshrining the ancestral tablets, which connect to the spirits of the departed of the family, female and male. The most important numinous, the sacred, in Chinese Religion is the family in and of itself. Family is understood to include the dead, the living, and the yet unborn. Also on the altar will be references to adjunct aspects of Chinese Religion, to be discussed below.

The relationship of the living and the dead is summed up in the concept, *xiao*. Essentially, *xiao* means that as parents nurture children, so children when they are grown nurture their parents, not only in old age, but after death. Food is offered to the deceased parents or grandparents in front of the spirit tablets on the household altar, as well as to the tablets of the clan ancestors in the clan temple, if the family is associated with one. The religious imperative is to continue the patrilineal family. On death one continues in the minds of the living members of

Figure 1 An altar in a Taiwan farming family home. To one side is a plaque with the names of the departed immediate family. In the middle is a small glass case with the images of Grandmother and Grandfather Earth, since it is a farming family. To the side are symbols of a religious society. Above on the wall (with the upper part cut off in the photograph) is the ubiquitous Guanyin (discussed in this chapter). In front of the name plaque and the images of the Earth deity couple are the ubiquitous altar furnishings: red lights or red candles, three cups for wine offerings, and a container to hold incense.

the family reinforced by the family tablets usually on view in the main room of the home and reified by the periodic offerings of food and wine.

The offering is a banquet of the best food the family can afford along with wine (tea for modern families oriented toward Buddhism) and sometimes entertainment. After the ancestral spirits have eaten the spiritual aspect of the food and drunk the wine, the living members of the family sit down and enjoy the physical aspects of the food. This banquet is normally held on the new and full moon of each lunar month and on all the festivals, especially the late winter Spring Festival ("Chinese New Year"). On one holiday in the spring, Qingming, the offering is made at the grave site, and the family enjoys a picnic there of the offered food.

As in many cultures, there is a concept of multiple souls. There are at least two (the number varies by time and region), one in the Sky with the souls of the family and clan connected to the living by the spirit tablet and one in Earth to which the family can connect with the souls of the departed at the grave or tomb.

Figure 2 Altar in clan temple in Taiwan with the name plaques of those ancestors who have most honored the clan. These altars are kept simple with only name plaques, aside from the usual altar furnishings. In front of the altar is the table on which the food offering will be laid out.

The offering not only has a religious function but a practical one as well. As Jews have their Sabbath meal on Friday evening and Christians tend to have a special Sunday dinner, so in Chinese Religion, these twice a month banquets ensure that people periodically eat highly nutritious food.

In many families today, an offering of incense and fruit is offered on the altar every morning. A marriage is solemnized by announcing the bride as a new member of the patrilocal family before the ancestral tablets; this is the only religious aspect of an otherwise social celebration: the wedding banquet. Similarly, births are similarly announced, as well as graduations, new jobs, etc.

The living and the dead exist in a reciprocal relationship. As the living care for the dead, so the dead support the welfare of the living from the spirit realm. If problems start to affect the family, a medium may be consulted, so the living can communicate directly with the dead through the possessed medium (discussed in Chapter 5).

(a)

(b)

Figures 3a and b Sweeping the tomb and laying out the food offerings during the Qingming Festival. Grave is of Southeastern Chinese style as found in Taiwan.

The *Classic of Xiao* cited above formalized these concepts thousands of years after they originated; written at first for the educated aristocracy, the literati or scholar-officials, as literacy spread, the book became a standard elementary text (it was the first I learned in studying literary Chinese). *Xiao* was understood to consist of five relationships (five becoming the sacred number in China replacing the earlier number six, as three is the sacred number in Indo-European language cultures). These relationships are parent and child, husband and wife, elder brother and younger brother, friends and ruler and government officials:

> Serving one's father and serving one's mother is similar in that it is done with love. Serving one's father and serving one's ruler is similar in that it is done with respect. Therefore, the mother brings forth love and the ruler brings forth respect, while the father brings forth both. Hence, serving the ruler with filiality elicits loyalty and serving elders with respect brings forth obedience. Being loyal and obedient to one's superiors leads to keeping one's rank and office and being able to continue the ritual offerings [to one's ancestors]. This is the filiality of the scholar-officials [earlier the term meant "knights"—chariot-riding aristocratic warriors]. (*Classic of Xiao*, chapter 5—own translation)

Xiao was formalized with the addition of loyalty to the ruler at the beginning of the first successful unification of the feuding Chinese kingdoms by the Han empire (the preceding unification of the Qin was short-lived; it collapsed after a single generation due to the unpopularity of the ruthlessly authoritarian regime). Hitherto, loyalty in the context of Familism had been to the clan head, which led to the fragmentation of China, as the many royal clans competed for hegemony. With unification, it was necessary to channel that clan loyalty toward the single ruler, the emperor, within the concept of *xiao*, Familism, itself.

But placing the relationship between the ruler and the ruled, between superior and inferior, within Familism meant that the ruler was constrained by Familism, and thus the ruler and his consort became known as the "Father and Mother of the People." As the people were to respect and be loyal to the ruler as to one's parents, so the ruler is to treat the people as his children, to nurture and love them in turn, to rule them with *ren*, perfect compassion. And a ruler who did not rule for the benefit of those he ruled was not a true ruler, and according to the foundational Confucian theorist, Mengzi, the ruler could be replaced; killing such a non-king was not then regicide.

When many centuries later, this concept of government was spread to Europe via the Jesuit "Relations" from China, it was revolutionary. Instead of the Christian Divine Right of Kings, here was the divine duty of kings to those he ruled. If a ruler did not rule for the benefit of the governed, revolution was legitimate. These ideas influenced Voltaire and Leibnitz, who in turn influenced Jefferson and Payne, leading to first the American and then the French revolutions against Divine Kingship, as implied by the wording of the American "Declaration of Independence."

While the ancestral spirits were the primary recipients of offering rituals, these were not the only spirits to whom ritual offerings were directed. These non-family spirits can be subsumed under the categories of cosmic spirits, weather spirits, geographic feature spirits, nature spirits, and the spirits of non-family powerful persons. Before introducing these spirits, however, it is necessary to digress to a discussion of the skewing of the Western translations and understandings of Chinese terms regarding divinities due to misogyny and the assumption that the Western understanding of religion based on Christianity is normative to all cultures.

The skewing of the Western understanding of Chinese deities due to ethnocentrism

The understanding of Chinese deities has been confused in the West for several reasons. One reason is the tendency of applying Western concepts of gender valuation, if not misogyny, to the Chinese concept of a harmonious balance between the genders, especially within the sphere of religion. A second reason is the assumption that Western monotheistic values are normative to the human psyche and therefore can be found in all cultures. The third reason is that the choice of Chinese terms for Western theological terms, even if misleading, are then reread back into Chinese texts, due to a false circular logic.

Two examples will be provided with regard to the first reason, one minor and one major. The minor example is the translation of the name for the most important Chinese deity around two thousand years ago: Xi Wang Mu (see Cahill 1993). The name literally translated is "West King Mother" or "King Mother of the West." But excepting myself, the name is invariably imprecisely translated "Queen Mother of the West," because She is female. While Indo-European Languages, such as English, are inflected—that is, words change according to gender, number, and tense—Chinese is not; gender, number and tense are indicated by the addition of extra words. Hence, the word *wang* (King) is not gendered; it applies to males and females. The Chinese have a word translated as "queen": *hou* (consort) which is used in the title of Mazu as

Queen of the Celestial Realm. Changing the name of the deity from "king" to "queen" renders the deity to be less important and powerful, often being but the consort of a ruler rather than a ruler in the Chinese sense of the word. As a corollary, when in the Tang dynasty, there was a female ruler, she had the title of "emperor" not "queen."

A more important example is the common Western attitude toward Earth as a deity. The primary cosmic deity is *Tiandi* (Sky-Earth), who as a couple, along with Yin and Yang, create all that exists. Sky-Earth is so supreme that in premodern times, only the emperor and his consort could make offerings to them; for anyone else to do so was understood as treason, because of usurping the prerogatives of the ruler of the world, China being *Zhongguo*, the Central State.

When the Jesuit missionaries reached Beijing (see Chapter 2), they lauded the offering to Sky but spoke against the offering to Earth, because it was female. They had created the Chinese term "Tianzhu" (Ruler of Sky) as the translation of God. Chinese intellectuals at the time objected, stating, "How can Tian (Sky) have a ruler, it being supreme," and further, "How can Tian alone create?" For the Chinese, as most humans in the world, save in the West, understand that creation requires both female and male inputs. For example, in Greek myths, Zeus gives birth to Dionysus, but he does so only after removing the embryo of Dionysus from the womb of Semele, whom Zeus had impregnated, and placing the embryo in his thigh.

Moreover, the standard translation of *Tiandi* is not "Sky-Earth" but "Heaven and Earth." But Tian means that which is above; it not only is the abode of one soul of the dead but also means "weather" and all that is observable in the Sky, such as the stars. "Heaven" has a different meaning entirely, being the abode of God, and the opposite of "Heaven" is not "Earth" but "Hell." In any case, only the male element in the compound is worthy of respect, not the female, so that even feminist sinologists have written "Heaven and earth," not "Heaven and Earth"! Furthermore, Christian missionaries told Chinese converts that their deceased parents and grandparents were in Hell because they had not been baptized. Thus, Chinese, even today understand that the English word for Di "Earth," with regard to the abode of one of the souls, is not "Earth" but "Hell," and so translate accordingly.

The third reason for the skewing of the understanding of Chinese Religion was the imposition of assumptions about the universality of Western religion. Thus, it tends to be assumed that all religions have if not a monotheistic deity, a "high god" or supreme deity.

Figure 4 Aside from the food and wine offering, Chinese send paper spirit money via fire to their ancestors to spend in the realm of the dead. To end the practice of burning large amounts of paper, the government encourages the practice of sending spirit credit cards, bank accounts, and checks that can be made out in large amounts instead. Also, the highly bureaucratic nature of traditional Chinese governance extended to the realm of the dead, who needed passports with the right stamps to enter the realm of the dead. There is a popular folk tale of a woman who died but was sent back to the realm of the living—came back to life—because she had the wrong stamp in her passport. It can be noted in the above passport, bankbook, credit card (modeled on the American Express card: "Don't leave life without it!"), and checks that the "Di" of "Tiandi" is translated into English as "Hell," since Sky-Earth is commonly translated as Heaven and Earth, but the opposite of Heaven is Hell, not Earth, and missionaries told Chinese Christians that their unbaptized parents were in Hell.

According to the written oracular material of the Shang dynasty, over three thousand years ago, offerings were made to Di and Shangdi. I am in agreement with some other scholars (e.g., Eno 1990b) that Di meant the aggregation of the dead spirits, and Shangdi, of the most powerful spirits, the spirits of the ruling clan. In other words, Shangdi is not a singular high god, but an assemblage of a number of spirits. Since the earlier Catholic missionaries had created the term Tianzhu (Ruler of Sky) to mean God, to be different, Protestant missionaries sought another word, and chose Shangdi as the Chinese term for God. Later Protestant translators, such as, for example, Karlgren, read the Protestant term back into the past and translated Shangdi as God—a beautiful example of circular logic—thus misleadingly positing a Western notion of God in early China.

A modern example of the West not just skewing Chinese values regarding gender (other than in regard to deities but with regard to religious values), but reversing them can be found in the 1998 Disney film, *Mulan*. Disney films are notorious for their negative treatment of non-Western cultures, such as *Aladdin* (1992), utterly disregarding non-Western sensibilities, such as *Pocahontas* (1995), or lauding slavery, as in *Song of the South* (1946). In *Mulan*, ultra-right conservative American values are projected as Chinese, in particular the consideration of women soldiers actually fighting as evil. Thus, in the Disney film, it is posited that a female found to be fighting as a soldier would be executed! But in China, the opposite is the case. There are many Chinese martial arts films in which the martial hero is female. Among early Chinese tombs, there are those for females full of weapons, indicating that the aristocratic woman entombed was a general. Mulan is a very popular Chinese folk hero who is seen as the epitome of *xiao*, because she took up her father's duties when he was too old and ill to answer the call to take up his general's position when China was attacked. Her story is taught in Taiwan schools as an example of *xiao* in action. Shaw Brothers (Hong Kong) produced a fine film of a *kunchu* opera based on the story: *Lady General Hua Mulan* (1964—available with English subtitles).

Cosmic deities

In the early sixteenth century, the Ming dynasty regime moved the capital from Nanjing ("Southern Capital" on the north bank of the Yangzi River) to Beijing ("Northern Capital" near the northern border). Aside from building the enormous palace (the "Forbidden City"), still in the center of the city, it built major altar establishments (large earthen platforms of tens of square meters with nearby buildings for preparation for the rituals). South of the city wall (the direction which the emperor faced while sitting on his throne) is the round, three tiered Altar to Sky (with the Temple to Good Harvests which combines over and over again the square symbol for Earth and the round symbol for Sky, nearby). North of the city is the Altar to Earth; east of the city, the Altar to Sun;

and west of the city, the Altar to Moon. To the west of the main gate to the palace is the Altar to Soil and Grain—this altar is to the spirit of the locale, and different from the sole Altar to Earth in the capital exclusively for offerings by the emperor; Altars to Soil and Grain will be found in all administrative centers, whether provincial of district. To the east, is the imperial clan temple, and, of course, in the center of the palace is the imperial family temple. All of these altars and temples are extant and can be visited, save for the Altar to Moon, on which was placed a radio tower during the Cultural Revolution, which was still there when I last visited it a couple of years ago. These altars were all for the exclusive offerings by the emperor (whose ritual moves were mirrored by the empress simultaneously within the palace grounds). The offerings were of silk and jade.

Aside from the Altar to Earth in the capital and the Altars to Soil and Grain in administrative centers in traditional times, ordinary people continue to make offerings to two different modes of Earth. Farming families often have a tiny shrine in which are images of Grandmother and Grandfather Earth in their farm fields and on the family altar. In this case, Earth is understood as a female-male pair, for fertility and generation of new plants naturally requires a female-male pairing.

Figure 5 Typical small agricultural field shrine housing images of Grandmother and Grandfather Earth. Bicycle indicates scale. Before the shrine are kneeling pads and a low platform for offerings. To the side is a furnace for burning spirit money.

The second mode is with regard to graves. Since the body is placed in Earth on burial, in many parts of China, by the side of the grave is a small shrine to the Lord of the Earth (Houtu), in whose care the body is entrusted and where resides one of the deceased souls.

Weather spirits

All agricultural societies are concerned about rain and, at least in premodern times, prayed to spirits for rain during droughts. China was no different. From the earliest times, we have records of rulers making offerings and praying to rain deities. These deities varied over time and region.

Geographic feature spirits

Again it is common in a number of traditions to consider particular mountains and bodies of water sacred. Aside from certain bodies of water, given the size of China a number of mountains were considered sacred. Most were considered so because famous Buddhist or Daoist monasteries or temples were located there—and usually they are very scenic—but some mountains were considered sacred in and of themselves. The most important such mountain is Taishan (the "Great Mountain").

Taishan is in northeast China, not far from the birthplace of Confucius. It is the only mountain in a large area and thus literally stands out. As far back as we have records, rulers made a pilgrimage there and made offerings to the deity of the mountain. A large number of temples of various sorts were built along the route to the top, which is paved with stones and there is a long, very wide, series of steps in the steeper, upper part. Today, large numbers of pilgrims make their way to the top making offerings at the various temples still extant on the way up, as well as those on the top. There is a town at its base with hotels and one can stay in some of the temples at the top. Tourists can take a bus halfway up and a cable car from there. But, if one wants to experience the mountain, it is best to join those making pilgrimage, often whole villages, stopping at the various temples along the way.

Other nature spirits

Aside from mountains and bodies of water, particular old trees and large rocks are considered sacred. One can recognize them, as usually there is a large red cloth sash tied around them, and before them there will be a container for incense for those making offerings.

Spirits of non-family powerful persons: *Shen* (Deities—can also mean non-deity spirits)

More than two thousand years ago, there were a number of deities that are now poorly understood. Some seem to have been part human and part animal, as found in other traditions, such as early Egypt, but our data from early texts is insufficient to clearly understand function and often appearance.

Mahayana Buddhism (see Chapter 8) introduced China to the notion of the Bodhisattva, a being whose accumulated merit is sufficient to attain nirvana but turns back from nonexistence until all living beings are ready for enlightenment. Thus Bodhisattvas are in a position to use their surplus merit to assist people and in China were perceived as saints in the Christian tradition: human spirits that can be prayed to for succor. Most *shen* are dead persons who can assist the living.

Typical of Familism traditions, mediumism (spirit possession) was an important feature of Chinese Religion (see Chapter 5). The earliest mode of mediumism was spirit possession by the family dead, especially in the elite offering rituals over two thousand years ago. Such possession allowed the recipient of the sacrifice to eat and drink via the possessed grandson or grand daughter-in-law and enabled the living to consult with the dead.

Because Chinese Religion is patrifocal, a female participated through the family into which she married; she was never a member of her natal family in the religious sense. Thus, an unbetrothed or unmarried female on death had no family to care for her. Under such circumstances, a family that could afford it would advertise for and pay a male to marry the girl's spirit, usually as a second wife. She would then be buried with his relatives and be cared for on his family altar. If this did not take place, she became an uncared for ghost, as did others who died under anomalous circumstances. Such ghosts had a penchant for possessing the living. If the possession was deemed to be maleficent, an exorcism was called for. But sometimes, the possession was benign, the ghost through the possessed person helping others. If such possession continued again with the same person or others, the ghost was understood to be a *shen*. Thus Chinese deities through possession could be spoken to, even touched, and faith was irrelevant when the deities could be directly apprehended and experienced.

There are a number of *shen*, whose importance varies with locale and function, who are too many to describe in this brief introduction. Readers are recommended to two easily read books for discussions of many of the deities, the classic study by Ke (1993) and a more recent one by Yang and An (2005). Three deities, however, will be introduced in the following to present some idea of the Chinese deities.

Guanyin (often called in English "The Goddess of Mercy") is found throughout China (see Yü 2001). Originally a male Bodhisattva called Avalokiteshvara, around a thousand years ago, he was transmuted into a female deity, called upon for succor in all sorts of situations and for residing in the Pure Land (see Chapter 8) upon death. She seems to have replaced the King Mother of the West. Aside from the many temples directed toward her, often attached to monasteries, She is commonly found as a picture behind and above family altars. She is ubiquitous, important not only to those oriented toward Buddhism, but to the general Chinese population as a whole.

In Taiwan, aside from Guanyin, the most important deity is Mazu. Among her many epithets, most common are Holy Celestial Mother and Queen of the Celestial Realm. Essentially She is a sea deity, especially important along coastal Fujian Province, the ancestral home of most Taiwanese. Her image is usually portrayed wearing the style of crown of two thousand years ago. A favorite of those who follow the sea, She is found in temples throughout Taiwan. It is to be noted that the biographies of these two goddesses point out that they are unmarried females.

My own favorite deity, because I keep running into him, so to speak, every time I am in Taiwan, is Jigong, who is known as the dipsomaniac deity, and is noted for his healing capability. A very popular deity, He is the subject of novels (see Shahar 1998) and more recently, films. He is generally portrayed in tattered Daoist robes (He is also listed as a Buddhist Arhat), holding a gourd filled with an alcoholic drink in one hand and a tattered fan in the other. I have often encountered mediums possessed by Him; in one instance, the possession was so powerful, I and the others around Him (that is the woman possessed by Him) powerfully felt we were in the presence of the sacred.

The process of deity formation is never-ending. A few years after Mao Zedong died, I noticed for sale everywhere amulets with a picture of Mao when young on one side and mature on the other. Hanging from the golden colored plastic frame was a plastic replica of a small Chinese gold ingot traditionally used for a large amount of currency. Hanging from that was a tiny bell, and below that

Figures 6a and b Small images of Jigong—one showing him in typical attire with fan and gourd, and the other a small folk pottery image showing him climbing out of a huge jar of wine (the label on the jar has the logograph for wine) with a marvelously amusing drunken look on his face. (Chinese do appreciate humor in their religion.)

a red tassel. It was meant to be hung from automobile rearview mirrors. To be certain my interpretation was correct, when I happened to be in a municipal government car in which the amulet was hanging, I asked the driver why it was there. He replied simply: "*Ta shih shen*" (He is a deity). When capitalism was declared to be the new economic model, a deity of capitalism was needed. Mao was a recently deceased powerful person and thus was available, and so he became the new deity of capitalism—irony of ironies. Chinese Religion is wondrously flexible.

Local temples

These *shen* are housed in non-family, non-clan temples which are available to everyone. Due to the clan social structure, there was no understanding of public space; village and urban neighborhood temples solved that problem. Such temples often housed a particular deity, represented by a large image, but local persons often brought smaller images of *shen* important to them to be placed there. Hence, a temple could house many *shen*. In front of the temple was usually a large space which functioned as small urban parks do today. There retired persons hung out with their friends, children played after school, people might play musical instruments or practice *taichi*. After rain, grain might be spread there to dry. The temple was overseen by a committee made up of individuals from local clans; there might be a paid caretaker, as well as someone selling necessities for approaching the *shen*, such as candles and spirit money, the profit going to the upkeep of the temple. But the one element common to Western churches not to be found would be a priest. Approaching the deities was simple and needed no intermediary. Sometimes Buddhist monasteries, especially in the West (such as Greater Toronto and Vancouver), might build a non-Buddhist temple on their premises for the local population, but the monks and nuns tend to stay clear of it, so as not to be seen as priests of the spirits placed there.

Many local temples were near or in markets. After purchasing food, shoppers would place the food on a long table in front of the temple for a short time as an offering, before bringing the food home. Uncooked food was offered at temples to *shen*; cooked food was offered before the family or clan altar and subsequently eaten by the living members of the family.

Figure 7 Neighborhood temple in the flamboyant Fujian style common to Taiwan.

Figure 8 Temple interior.

Shen were not only offered food and drink but entertainment as well. Across the open space in front of many temples, there is a stage for operas facing the deities. Itinerant opera groups could be commissioned to put on an opera. Theoretically, the opera was being performed to entertain the *shen*, but, of course, all the local people crowded into the space to enjoy the opera. When television first came to Taiwan, a TV set would be placed facing the deities, but everyone in the community could thus watch the programs.

Large temples would house several major deities, and those who had need would make offerings and request to all in turn. If the request was successful, then offerings were again made to all, as one could not be certain which of the deities was responsible. If a temple was resplendent, it was a sign that many people had their needs fulfilled and made gifts to the temple; if a temple was in disrepair, probably people felt unfulfilled and sought succor at another temple.

Temples, large and small, had various implements for foretelling the future and making important decisions. These were frequently used for all sorts of reasons. Some temples had mediums on call for either healing or prognostication.

Small shrines to *shen* housing deities especially important for success in business will be found in stores and restaurants. These are for the benefit of the proprietor.

Figure 9 Gathering in front of larger temple.

Figure 10 Prognostication paraphernalia: small curved wooden blocks are thrown and read by whether they fall up or downside; a container of thin wooden rods is shaken until one flies out—the number on it is matched to a printed prognosis on the wall.

Figure 11 Shrine in small store.

Figure 12 Shop selling images of *shen*.

Daoism

No English term regarding religion in China is more misunderstood than Daoism (Taoism). This is because the term is used to translate two related but different Chinese concepts—*Daojia* and *Daojiao*—and these different concepts tend to be confused.

Daojia, often perceived as "philosophical Daoism," refers to one of the schools of thought of the late Zhou period, over two thousand years ago. Literally, it is a bibliographic term from the first library relating to three books housed (*jia*) together: the *Zhuangzi*, the *Daodejing* (or *Laozi*) and the *Liehzi*. The earliest part of the first of these was written by Zhuang Zhou in the fourth century BCE (for translation see Watson 1968, for analysis, see Paper 1995b: Chapter 5 or Paper 2004: 89–97). The work begins with a discussion of the mystic experience and later parts reinterpret the terms relevant to the experience to sociopolitical concerns, the main intellectual concern 2,200 years ago. The second book (see Lau 1963 for translation), probably compiled in the third century BCE, has been translated into English more often than any other book in any language. This in part is because the work is very short (300 brief passages) and thus those who barely can read Chinese assume they can translate a very difficult text. Usually one can perceive whether the translation is worthwhile by the first line which is often misconstrued. Western readers tend to assume the book is about mysticism, when actually it is a book about political control. The third book (see Graham 1960 for translation) is a book of diverse stories and anecdotes that has had little impact on the West, different from the previous two. None of these works are directly pertinent to Chinese Religion.

Daojiao, which literally means "the teachings of the Dao" or "Daoist teachings," is often understood in the West to mean Daoist religion. It is an institutionalized esoteric religion, differing from Chinese Religion which is a diffuse religion, whose complexity precludes a meaningful discussion in a short space. But a number of excellent scholars, including Westerners who are initiated Daoist priests, have been producing important introductory studies of this esoteric tradition for the last several decades. Readers are recommended to Langerway 1987; Saso 1972, 1978, and 1990; and Schipper 1993 (1982).

The establishment of the main Daoist sects is most complex and somewhat controversial. On the one hand, they are influenced by the beginning of Buddhism in China to varying degrees, and on the other hand, their roots are much earlier than the entry of Buddhism. As the Han dynasty was collapsing in the second century CE, various factions in the government struggled for power and were decimated by their rivals. One such faction was the *fangshi*, the court exorcists and controllers of the spiritual realm. Losing political power, some formed a religio-political movement, the Five Pecks of Rice or Yellow Turbans, who nearly succeeded in militarily overthrowing the government. Putting the insurrection down let to the demise of the weakened Han dynasty, as the general of the army put his son on the throne of a new dynasty. The remnant leaders of the Yellow Turbans seem to have begun institutional Daoism.

Daoism is a religion unlike the Western ones, as it is integrated, along with Buddhism, into the Chinese religious gestalt. Sometimes my Western students informed me that they were a Daoist, not realizing that it is not a church one joins. In China, those who are called Daoists are either initiated priests, often of a family of hereditary priests, or monks or nuns; there are no lay Daoists. The priests, usually part-time, are called upon for elaborate funeral rituals or periodic community renewal rituals when they wear elaborate robes. They are specialists in communicating with the spiritual realm. Monks and nuns focus on practices leading to the extension of life, as well as over time making the body ephemeral and becoming a *xian*, in this case, meaning a being of pure spirit. Daoism has its own pantheon of deities, some also claimed by Buddhism, with the Jade Emperor at the apex.

The Chinese government only recognizes five religions: Buddhism, Daoism, Islam, Protestantism and Catholicism (because Christian missionaries denied their sectarian rival was Christian, Chinese tend to assume the latter two are separate religions with nothing in common). Although the Russian Orthodox Church is present on their long border with Russia, and there was a Chinese Judaism (see Chapter 9), neither Orthodox Christianity nor Judaism is recognized as a religion by the present Chinese government. Chinese Religion is termed "folklore" rather than a religion. Thus, of the five recognized religion, only Daoism is purely Chinese, and local temples are called Daoist for lack of any other recognized appellation, even though there is no resident priest and the deities enshrined may have nothing to do with Daoism. Needless to add, it is understandable why so many Western tourists are quite confused in this regard.

Synthesis in Chinese Religion: Funerals

Buddhism and Daoism are institutional religions separate from the state as a religious institution (see Chapter 6) that have over the centuries accommodated themselves to function as adjuncts to Chinese Religion and culture as a seamless whole. This is why there is no conflict between them as there once was (see

Chapter 8). On a less important level, another accommodation can be found in Buddhist and Daoist monasteries built on scenic mountains serving as hostels for tourists. More importantly, especially in Taiwan, both serve in the transition of the dead to family spirits, that is, funeral rituals.

Daoist priests are hired to officiate at funerals, often presenting elaborate mime dramas of delivering documents about the dead person to the underworld hierarchy. More recently, they have added the role of modern funeral directors, offering for purchase all the necessities for funerals.

Paper representations, often artfully done, are burned to send both the necessities for life and of luxuries, for the enjoyment of the dead. One can buy paper suites of clothes for both sexes, eyeglasses, make-up paraphernalia, luxury cars, computers, DVD players, and fully furnished comfortable dwellings.

Buddhist monks or nuns are hired to say masses for the dead after funerals and on certain anniversaries of the death. The income from saying masses is how these Buddhists support themselves, as they pay for their keep at the monasteries.

Figure 13 Daoist priest officiating at a funeral.

Figure 14 Model of a furnished house made of bamboo strips for support and paper.

Figure 15 Buddhist nuns chanting sutras before an image of the deceased (a storefront has been cleared for the funeral).

Synthesis in intellectual history: *Sanjiao* (Three Teachings)

The Chinese ideal in political and social life is harmony. As the primary religious traditions of China have long ago harmonized into virtually a single construct, so too the intellectual streams of Chinese thought have also been harmonized. Prior to the Han dynasty, in the late first millennium BCE, there were numerous schools of thought. As the Han succeeded in creating a homogeneous religion and culture to ensure a stable China, leading intellectuals brought together the various strains of thought into a single, multifaceted intellectual system called *rujia*, an untranslatable term referring to the ever-changing ideology of the government bureaucracy of the time, misleadingly translated as "Confucianism."

Following the internationally cosmopolitan Tang dynasty, in which various concepts and other aspects of life were adopted from the West, South Asia, and Persia, the Song dynasty in the tenth century again began a process of integrating the various modes of thought, especially aspects of Chan (Japanese: Zen) Buddhism and Daojia into a revivified *rujia*, termed in the West, "Neo-Confucianism." At this time too, with a strengthened civil service system based on examinations of the literati, the literati developed *wen miao* ("civil"or

Figure 16 Students practicing the dance they will perform at the annual offering to Kongzi (Confucius) at the *wen miao*; it is called the Temple to the First Teacher in Taipei, Taiwan.

Figure 17 At the *wen miao* in Pingyao, China, one can see a large number of hanging red emblems, each signifying the making of an offering by a student.

Figure 18 Image of Mazu in her full regalia as Queen of Sky (Heaven).

Figure 19 The interior of the first court of the largest temple in Taiwan, perhaps the largest Chinese temple in the world, housing the oldest image of Mazu on the island.

"literati" temples—see Chapter 6). These temples housed name plaques of the founders of Chinese sociopolitical thought to which offerings were made at the birthday of Kongzi (Confucius), classrooms for secondary education, and examination halls for the civil service examinations. They also had an important function of being a clubhouse for the literati (those who had at least passed the first of the three examinations).

In modern times, the *wen miao* has also become a temple where students pray for success in the university entrance examinations.

By at least a thousand years ago, Buddhism, Daoism, and the *rujia* tradition were called the *sanjiao*, the "Three Teachings," but invariably the term was used in the statement that "The Three Teachings are one," meaning that the three are understood to be harmonized into a single ideological construct and that the three complement each other into a harmonious whole. This will become a major source of Western misunderstanding as will be discussed in the next chapter.

Chinese tend not to distinguish between temples belonging to the various *jiao* (religious modalities in this sense of the term). Whichever temple they go to, they pray for spiritual aid in their various endeavors, whether it be passing examinations, success in business, having a male heir, and so forth. Hence, their behavior tends to be the same at each, as all are in a sense Buddhist, Daoist, and Confucian.

2

Five Centuries of Western Misrepresentation of Chinese Religion

The fallacy of "Three Chinese Religions"

. . . my first visit to Taiwan. I had assumed Chinese people would categorize
their own religious beliefs much as we did . . . all Chinese, I had reasoned would
similarly be Buddhist, Daoist, or Confucian. To my surprise, none of the people
I met identified themselves as such. And, as far as I could tell, they all attended
the same Buddhist, Daoist, and popular religious temples. (Hansen 1990: ix)

On my first visit to Taiwan in 1965, I had the good fortune to be invited as a
guest to a bimonthly offering in a family home, which led me to realize that
virtually everything I had read on religion in China, and I had read extensively,
was either wrong or misleading. On the longer form of the Canadian census
which does ask about religion, almost all Chinese in Canada, save for Christians,
chose "none" from the list of religions. This is because they could find no term
with which they could identify, since few if any consider themselves Buddhist,
Daoist, or Confucian. Why is this?

The problem began a half-millennium ago. Matteo Ricci, an Italian Jesuit,
was the first Christian missionary to enter China in centuries. He reached
Portuguese Macao in 1582. There he studied not only spoken Chinese but the
literary language. Being a monk, at first he thought to wear the garb of Chinese
Buddhist monks. But he soon discovered that monks were popularly held in
disrepute (see Chapter 8) and, having become learned in the literati tradition,
took on the clothing of the literati. In 1601, he received permission to move to
Beijing, the capital, where his knowledge of Western astronomy and mapmaking
was much appreciated. Soon, fellow Jesuits arrived and accepted government
positions in the Bureau of Astronomy/Astrology.

The Jesuit mode of missionizing was different from other Christian missionaries, as they sought to convert those at the top of society and government, hoping that their Christianity would then filter down to ordinary people. Franciscan and Dominican missionaries, who arrived somewhat later, sought to convert the masses and disagreed with the Jesuits in a number of regards (see Chapter 8).

Wherever they missionized, the Jesuits wrote *Relations* back to European intellectuals, describing the cultures in which they lived. With regard to Chinese Religion, the Jesuits were faced with two dilemmas. The first dilemma was that it was understood in Europe that Christian converts could not continue their previous religious practices, which were ipso facto Heathen and consequently forbidden. The Jesuits had been moderately successful in converting several imperial princes and a few high officials to Christianity. But the Jesuits did not ask them to cease participating in family, clan, and state rituals. For if they did, they would have lost their sense of their own identity (see Chapter 4) and their government positions.

The second dilemma was that Jesuits were accepting government positions, which meant they would be expected to take part, in a limited way, in state rituals. Explicit official appointment began with Johann Adam von Schall after the Manchu occupation of the capital, and the Papacy eventually authorized Jesuits to hold such offices. But the Roman Catholic Church of Ricci's time, within a century of the expulsion of Muslims and Jews from Spain, had zero tolerance for participating in non-Christian rituals and executed those convicted of such participation. For example, a Spanish trader at this time in what is now the southeastern United States was charged with heresy by the Inquisition for participating in those Native American rituals essential for trade and burned at the stake (see Kessell 1978).

A third problem that has to be dealt with in the *Relations* was to justify support for their mission. They did this by describing Chinese culture and religion as being proto-monotheistic and therefore ready and willing to accept the Christian truth of a triune monotheism. In Ricci's erroneous presentation, Chinese polytheism, with its focus on ancestral and ghost spirits and the complementary dualistic female Earth-male Sky non-anthropomorphic deities, was subsidiary to a male singular high god:

> From the very beginning of their history it is recorded that they recognized and worshiped one Supreme Being whom they called the King of Heaven, or designated by some other name indicating his rule over heaven and earth. (Ricci 1953: 93)

To solve his dilemmas, Ricci interpreted *sanjiao* ("Three Teachings") to mean three religious sects: Buddhism, Daoism, and Confucianism. Hence, Ricci found religious pluralism where there was none. Ricci was well aware that his understanding was not the Chinese one:

> The most common opinion today among those who believe themselves to be the most wise is to say that these three sects are one and the same thing and can be observed at once. By this they deceive themselves and others too. (Fontani Ricciani I, 32 in Gernet 1985: 64)

The Jesuits declared Confucianism to be a religion compatible with Christianity but missing the element of the Trinity. So the Chinese elite were ready and waiting for the Christian truth, thus arguing for the continuation of support for their mission.

Ricci was adamant that the literati only adhered to the Confucian "sect" and would never "belong to any other sect." He apparently was completely oblivious to the important role of Daoist and Buddhist ideology and practices among the elite, as is normative, for example, in literati aesthetics. More importantly, the term *sanjiao*, in effect, excludes the vast majority of Chinese religious behavior: the offering complex found at all levels of society. Thus, his reporting turned a blind eye to normative Chinese Religion at both the clan and state level, and thus he and his converts could not be perceived as practicing non-Christian religious rituals.

Ricci's sixteenth century deliberately false description became a religious studies dogma, persisting to this day. This understanding was reinforced in the last century by Soothill's popular volume, *The Three Religions of China*, first published in 1913. It begins, "There are three recognized religions in China . . . and the three religions may be considered as three aspects of the established religion of the country." The latter phrase, as well as its inconsistency with the former, has been ignored by the authors of world religions textbooks, where the "fact" of three religions in China is a virtual constant. Texts treating Chinese Religion as singular were not published until the mid-twentieth century, the most important being Laurence Thompson's, *Chinese Religion, An Introduction*, first published in 1969 (see Girardot 1992):

> Our use of the word religion in the singular is intended, then, to convey our interpretation that the character of religious expression in China is above all a manifestation of Chinese culture. To attempt to understand religion in China as several systems of doctrine is to read Western experience into a quite different set of circumstances. (L. Thompson 1989: 1)

My own book (Paper 1995b), followed Thompson's lead. Unfortunately, while most specialists in religion in China understand a singular religious gestalt in China, this understanding has not spread to scholars of religion in general. Even recent books on religion in China continue to promote the "three religions in China" dogma; for example, McDermott 2011. And some world religion textbooks continue this false presentation, as Adler 2002, Poceski 2009 and Fowler and Fowler 2008. (For an extended analysis of this topic, see Paper 1995b: Chapters 1 and 2.)

On the popular level in the West, there seems to be a non-Chinese universal understanding that Chinese are Buddhists. My wife is Chinese, and my parents on meeting her assumed that she was, although she knew virtually nothing about Buddhism. I have heard people over and over again make that assumption. Yet neither she nor any of her family, nor any of her friends, would so identify themselves. Indeed, until she became aware of the study of Chinese Religion as singular, she did not have a term for what has been a no-name religion.

Until the West has a better understanding of the foundation of Chinese culture, that is, Chinese Religion, relations between the West and China are doomed to dangerous misunderstandings. Hence, the misunderstanding of Chinese communism, which maintains the values of Chinese Religion, if not its rituals, and is quite different from Russian communism (Stalin hated Chinese communism and supported the Nationalist Party along with the United States during the Civil War). This misunderstanding had encouraged if not led to the expansion of the Korean War and the American takeover of the war in Vietnam from the French, resulting in the deaths of millions (see Chapter 7 for further discussion of these points).

Relevant cognitive and neurological studies

There is a continuing attempt to use neuropsychology and cognitive studies to scientifically prove the truth and universality of Christian theology and that it is embedded in the human brain. Among the earliest to write on the topic was the neurologist Eugene d'Aquili who sought to find "God in the brain." His publications stretched over two decades. In his last work, coauthored with Andrew Newberg (1999: 67), it is stated that in all religions, "the concepts of a Christ figure or a solar hero represent cognitive solutions within the myth [in general] to the problem of the basically autonomous myth structure."

The application of cognitive studies by some scholars continues to promote an ethnocentric understanding of religion applied universally to all persons and societies (Clark and Winslett 2011: 932 [for a rejoinder, see Paper 2012b]):

> Cognitive science of religion holds that religious belief is natural and will routinely take characteristic shapes and forms. The evolutionary psychology of religion suggests that religious beliefs that have been channeled into moralizing high gods can effectively overcome human selfishness necessary for the gain of cooperative benefits. Taken together, they suggest that successful human groups, including those in ancient China, will likely and repeatedly develop beliefs in high, moralizing, providential gods who exercise moral providence.

I have been countering such anti-comparative theological standpoints for decades, beginning with "The Post-Contact Origin of An American Indian High God" in 1983 (see also Paper 2007: Chapter 3 "Theology"). I have also argued that in most polytheistic traditions, the deities are morally neutral. In these cultures, it is humans rather than the deities who carry out divinely assisted actions and societies which determine whether these acts are good or bad, not the deities. Consequently, society not divinity punishes those perceived to be a danger to the social body (see Paper 2005).

There are sufficient archaeological finds to indicate that human cultures since their beginning have had an understanding of and means for interacting with the numinous. It is the stance that the specifics of this understanding are worldwide that is being disputed. This chapter, in part, is an attempt to argue that specific theologies are not universal and that, for example, the theology of the early Chinese elite continuing today among all Chinese following their traditional religion has an understanding of the numinous very different from the Christian understanding(s); that is, the Christian theological paradigm cannot be used for religion in general.

It is not that neurological and cognitive studies cannot assist us in understanding the similarities and differences between theologies. But to start one's study with ethnocentric premises is contrary to the scientific method which should examine phenomena without a priori assumptions, although such assumptions are often unconscious. There are scholars involved with the cognitive study of religion who do place primacy on the evidence and theorize from what the evidence suggests, rather than on ethnocentric theological universals.

At the archaeological site of Çatalhöyük in Anatolia, several seminars have taken place with archaeologists, ethnologists, theologians, and comparative religionists, and two volumes of their papers have been published to date

(Hodder 2010, 2014a). F. Leron Shults, a theologian whose research interest is the cognitive science of religion, emphatically states that "The people of Çatalhöyük were clearly not monotheists" (2014a: 77). Instead, the anthropologist of religion and one of the founders of the cognitive science of religion, Stewart Elliot Guthrie, writes, "Religion at Çatalhöyük featured relations with deceased ancestors and other nonhuman persons" (2014: 102–3). The consequences of this religious focus is pointed out by another theologian interested in the interaction between religion and science, J. Wentzel van Huyssteen: "What is clear at Çatalhöyük, however, is that notions of self were directly bound up with the house and were continuous with ancestors and other beings and things" (2014: 120–21). All would agree that rituals directed toward ancestors and other nonhuman persons were the bonds that held society together, not fear of a punitive deity. The moderator of the seminars, the archaeologist Ian Hodder, sums up: "The ancestors and the wild bull were the foci around which social groups formed and developed relations with each other" (2014b: 3) These understandings, without reference to "the wild bull," are precisely the basis of Chinese theology, as well as its bearing on society and the individual, and indicate its very long time depth to the beginnings of horticulture.

Linguistic studies and neurological science can also assist in understanding the difference between Chinese Religion and the major Western religion. A half-century ago, Nakamura (1964) proposed that language influences cognition, both in perception and reasoning. Regarding the difference between the philosophy of cultures that speak Indo-European languages (such as Sanskrit, Greek, Latin, and English), and Chinese philosophy, the latter is comparatively pragmatic, and Chinese thinking avoids non-specific universals, such as Truth and Beauty. In part this can be understood with regard to the different priority the brain gives to the senses with regard to sight and sound; logographic writing uses the visual part of the brain, while alphabetic writing uses the aural. Nakamura's analysis has been verified by later neurological studies which have demonstrated that alphabetic and logographic written languages utilize different parts of the brain and this in turn leads to different modes of cogitation even with regard to non-literary thinking, such as arithmetic (Tan et al. 2000, 2001; Tang et al. 2006).

From these studies, one would not be surprised to find that theological entities in Indo-European cultures tend to be intangible and later may become absolute, as in the monotheistic traditions, while in logographic language cultures, such as China, theological beings are tangible and not absolute. For at least the last thousand years, those *shen* who are deceased non-family human deities are known through their possessing mediums, some even writing their autobiographies through possessed literati. Thus Chinese are able to directly speak to, be healed by, read books by, and touch and be touched by their deities. Hence, we do not find monotheism in China. When high gods do appear in China, as in institutionalized Daoism, they follow the bureaucratic model of the Chinese imperial government, which is quite different from the older history of religions' notion of high gods (see entry "High God" in the online *Encyclopædia Britannica* 2015).

I am not the only Sinologist who has noted the ethnocentric bias of the new cognitive studies of religion. Harold Roth (2008), for example, has also argued that the cognitive approach is often a matter of unreflective ethnocentrism and cognitive imperialism, and Pan (2017) has countered other cognitive arguments regarding Chinese culture by Edward Slingerland. The problem with cognitive studies of religion in these regards is that many are constructed from databases that are composed of these earlier studies of Chinese and other religions that often have little if any validity. Using these unreliable databases, one can seemingly prove virtually any point one may wish about the nature of religion globally.

3

Familism: The Global Context of Chinese Religion

Prologue

This chapter is divided into two parts. The first part, continuing the previous chapter, discusses how Chinese Religion has been misunderstood due to the widespread use of Christianity as a model for religion in general, aspects on which I and others have written a number of times. The second part suggests an alternative model for understanding Chinese and many other similar religions; this part presents a new model for the study of religion not only in China but in general.

I am hardly alone in critiquing ethnocentrism in the study of religion. Two books are outstanding with regard to dealing with the issues discussed in the following. The year 1998 saw the publication of Daniel Dubuisson's *L'Occident et la religion: Myths, science et idéologie* (published in English translation as *The Western Construction of Religion* in 2003) which presents in far greater depth some of the issues discussed below. In 2000, Timothy Fitzgerald's *The Ideology of Religious Studies* was published; this as well as his later works have elicited a large number of rejoinders from other religious studies scholars, leading to a still continuing conversation. A specialist in non-Western religions, Fitzgerald has run into similar conceptual problems as I have, and as Dubuisson, provides a history of the problems and discusses some, such as Ninian Smart, who can be understood as unconsciously perpetuating an ethnocentric, indeed a Christocentric, approach to the study of religion.

Part 1: The Christian imposition on the understanding of Chinese Religion

Introduction

Because of Christian missionizing, Chinese Religion has remained virtually invisible both to scholars and governments inside and outside of China for dual reasons. The first reason is due to the needs and attitudes of Christian missionaries for the last half millennium who either deliberately falsified Chinese Religion or deemed it ignorant superstition, as well as the work of the Devil. The second reason is that religious studies began as essential knowledge for Christian missionaries, and even when secularized a half-century ago, continues to delineate religion according to the model of Christianity. Both approaches either deliberately served the colonial enterprise or are an instance of the continuation of a colonial attitude, even if unconscious, toward other cultures.

By Chinese Religion, as discussed in Chapter 1, I am referring to the religion based on *jing zu* (reverencing ancestors) in the Chinese mode. This foundational core is summed up by an aphorism that already was archaic when it was inserted into the beginning of the *Lunyu* (I,9) 2,500 or so years ago: *shen zhong zhui yuan* ("Carefully attend to the last [rites of parents] and follow up when [they are] long gone [with offerings]"). As previously delineated, Chinese Religion is based on the understanding of the family and clan as numinous, as well as the model for society and government. The primary ritual is the offering of a meal to the departed to be shared by the living. Individuals are subordinated to family, and life after death is based on the understanding of family as including the past and future members of the family. The religious imperative is to have sons (now moving toward daughters as well) to carry on the family line.

This central aspect has been synthesized with the worship of deities, and Buddhism and Daoism have become major adjuncts. In other words, religious modalities in China aside from the central core focusing on family should not be understood as separate religions, but as serving to enhance this core, even though they are carried on outside of the family and clan structures, in temples, monasteries, etc. As will be discussed later, some initially functioned separately, but only those that synthesized with family rituals survived over the many centuries. To use the Chinese metaphor of trunk and branches, Chinese Religion is the trunk and the various regional variations, as well as the adjunct religions, are the branches. To continue the metaphor, the root of the tree is the global religion of Familism (*zuxianjiao*) that will be introduced in the second part of this paper.

It is important to point out that the problem in coming to terms with religion in China is not a problem for current specialists in Chinese Religion or religion in China. Rather it is a problem for those in religious studies in China and Taiwan who are unfamiliar with the realities of Chinese Religion and history or who have not realized that their own personal and family experiences are relevant, and for those in government who are trying to manage religion in China, and to a lesser extent in Taiwan, while not according authenticity to the fundamental Chinese mode of religious expression. Moreover, it is a problem in North America as the religion of ethnic Chinese are not accorded recognition, and therefore legitimacy, by the Canadian and US governments (see Lai, Paper and Paper 2005: 89–110).

The Christian missionary understanding of Chinese Religion

The understanding of normative Chinese Religion, when it is recognized at all, maintains that it is superstition to be replaced by Western thinking. Thus, it is called a "folk religion," meaning the ignorant religion of an uneducated, barely civilized people. Tellingly, the term "folk religion" is virtually only applied to Chinese Religion, as a perusal of internet search engines will verify. Hinduism (literally the religion of the Indus River Valley), also a foreign construct, is not called a folk religion because the British colonized South Asia primarily for economic not ideological reasons, and Christian missionary activity was discouraged by the English East India Company so as not to further upset the population and threaten the corporation's profits. Hence, Hinduism, rather than being considered superstition, ended up being romantically idealized by many British people and Americans.

Calling Chinese Religion a folk religion derogates Chinese Religion and is logically absurd, as it is the very opposite of a folk religion. The essential features of Chinese Religion were the prerogative of the aristocratic clans in the proto-historic period. Only in the Han period, two thousand years ago, did the non-elite come to have family names and thus directly participate in Chinese Religion. Moreover, the central rituals of the emperor and empress up to a century ago were identical with the primary rituals of the peasantry, save being considerably more elaborate. The heads of provinces and districts had governmental as well as priestly functions (see Chapter 6). In the provincial and district government quarters, there were several temples where the officials led rituals for the benefit of the region and to celebrate literati culture.

A modern replacement for "folk religion" is "popular religion," which is often applied to Chinese Religion in scholarly writing. According to *A New Dictionary of Religions*:

> There is no single definition of what constitutes "Popular Religion." Some scholars have defined it as rural in contrast to urban forms of religion, the religion of the peasant in contrast to that of the ruling classes; or, in a variation of this definition, the religion of the masses as contrasted with that of the intellectual or sophisticated classes. If, however, popular religion is seen in contrast to "official" religion, the latter defined as religion founded on authoritative documents and propagated and maintained by religious specialists, priests or hierarchy, then the term "popular" can apply to any layperson, whether peasant or ruling-class, who adopts beliefs and practices which may be at odds with the religious specialist's views.

Of course, none of these meanings are relevant to Chinese Religion. Thus, the term, probably unwittingly for most scholars who use it, perpetuates the Christian missionary contempt for Chinese Religion and Chinese culture.

Hence, a current Chinese term to designate Chinese Religion, *minjian zongjiao*, when referring to Chinese culture, should not be translated as "folk religion" or "popular religion," both of which imply the religion of the uneducated or religion other than the mainstream religion of the culture, but should be translated as "Chinese [Han] ethnic religion." "Ethnic" in this usage means the characteristics of a people or culture. It should be noted that the term *minjian zongjiao* copied the Japanese usage, as did the term for religion itself, *zongjiao*, and many of these borrowings poorly fit the Chinese language context and have caused much confusion over the years.

The development of religious studies

The earliest students of comparative religion were the Jesuits, who wrote their *Relations* to Europe from their missionary centers in (present-day) China, Canada, and Paraguay describing the religion and other features of non-Western cultures as they perceived them. Eventually, non-Western religions began to be taught in divinity schools, institutes for the training of Protestant ministers and missionaries. Within European and American universities, it was taught under the umbrella of knowing the enemy to better convert the "natives." As late as 1960, when I wished to study comparative religion in the Divinity School of the University of Chicago under the tutelage of Eliade and Kitagawa, I had to leave after a year because as a non-Christian I could not honestly pass the faith-based examinations designed for the Christian ministry required before one could specialize in non-Christian religions. As I discovered, the same requirement was also to be found at such universities as Harvard and Princeton. Accordingly, I shifted to the study of classical Sinology with a focus on intellectual history. When I was able to move back into religious studies in the early 1970s, I approached religion not from a Christian or even a Western perspective but from a Chinese one. This allowed me to more readily perceive Native American and African religions than my colleagues trained in divinity schools, and these studies, in turn, further heightened my understanding of Chinese Religion.

The religious studies situation only began to change in the mid-1960s with the development of religious studies programs in state-supported American universities. But even in the 1970s at the University of Toronto, for example, those who taught East Asian religions were retired Christian missionaries from China and Japan, and one was replaced following retirement by a former Catholic nun with close ties to an influential European Catholic theologian. She was a major influence on turning the Center for World Religions at the Chinese Academy for the Social Sciences for a while toward Christian theology rather than religious studies—the two fields considered distinctly separate in the West.

Thus, students who came out of these programs were indoctrinated to understand religion from a Christian perspective, often without understanding the degree of the indoctrination and how it influenced their understanding of non-Christian religions. With regard to Chinese Religion, a change took place beginning in the 1960s when scholars began to either intensively study literary, Daoist and/or Buddhist Chinese, and thus begin to think in Chinese terms, or became fluent in spoken Chinese and studied Chinese Religion in situ, that is, did actual fieldwork, particularly in Taiwan, and perceived how Chinese live their religion. Most Western scholars of religion in China now do understand Chinese Religion, but this understanding has not by and large influenced contemporary Chinese thinking on religion in their own culture which depends on a non-Chinese Christian model.

The contemporary rise of fundamentalism in the monotheistic traditions, however, is now having an impact on some Western scholars of Chinese civilization. As discussed in the previous chapter, a classical Sinologist working with a Protestant theologian has understood the new cognitive science of religion to posit as a fact that "a high, moralizing god with strategic knowledge who exercises a kind of high moral providence"—that is, the God of the Hebrew Bible—is an essential feature of human cognition in all cultures.

Defining religion according to the Christian Model and its relationship to Chinese Religion

The effect of studying non-Western religion through a Christian lens is to understand religion both in general and in various cultures on the model of Christianity. But Christianity, as I will argue, is an anomaly among religions worldwide and is so idiosyncratic that it is the worst possible model for understanding religion globally. I am hardly alone in these criticisms, yet they seem to have little impact. Joseph Kitagawa, an Episcopal priest and one of the founders of the influential journal, *History of Religions*, made a critique similar to my own of the same year (1991) several decades ago:

> The East Asian universe has not been well understood by Western scholars because none of the alternative "implicit paradigms" of religion usually familiar to Westerners is readily applicable to East Asian traditions. It should be noted in this connection that "implicit paradigms" of religion does not refer to any explicit system of creed or cult but, rather, to an almost intuitive sense of the shape and contour of what religion is. (1991: 85)

An analysis of Christianity presents at least twelve determining factors, most of which are unique to Christianity:

Belief

Belief is fundamental to Christianity in general (and is crucial to most Protestant traditions in distinction to Catholicism as it understands salvation by faith alone) because adherence to a creed is essential to membership, especially the belief in a triune, singular deity, which is inherently illogical and thus requires faith. Hence, most dictionary definitions of religion focus on belief. Religions are often called "faith traditions." No other religious tradition centers on faith. For example, in Judaism, behavior—performing *mitzvah*—is far more important than belief. If one accepts the existence of God, which is not required, then God is necessarily understood to be singular. This is acceptance rather than belief. In Chinese Religion, belief is utterly meaningless, because knowing one has parents and grandparents, the numinous focus, is not a matter of faith but basic knowledge learned in infancy. A relatively recent Supreme Court of Canada decision defined religion solely by individual belief (*Syndicat Northcrest v. Amselem* [2004] 2 SCR 551). Thus, now in Canada there is freedom of belief but not necessarily freedom of religious behavior or practices without belief in the Christian sense, and this has resulted in the denial by the Supreme Court of the validity of major aspects of indigenous religion (*Ktunaxa Nation v. British Columbia* [2017] 2 SCR 386).

For over a century, students of religion have argued that belief should not be considered essential to understanding religions. This position had been well summarized by Jason N. Blum in an excellent study examining the issue:

> Among the various problems with belief, perhaps those that are most familiar to scholars of religion concern the historical origin of the category and the often implicit assumption that belief is the "essence of religion." In short, the notion that belief constitutes the necessary quality or most important aspect of religion appears to be a particular Christian—and more specifically, a modern, Protestant Christian—idea (Schilbrack 2014: 58). Because other religions do not necessarily emphasize belief, this has resulted in fundamentally misconstruing those traditions and misleading the entire discipline (as well as the public) into conceiving of religion as principally a matter of what people believe. . . . There is, therefore, widespread recognition that positing belief as the central category of religions does violence to non-Christian religions. (Blum 2018: 644–45)

The above is not to suggest that belief does not exist in Chinese Religion, only that it is not central to or a determining aspect of the religion. While I have never met anyone making offerings to ancestors who believe that the ancestral spirits actually eat the spiritual essence of the offered food, there seems to be a vague belief that the ancestors do exist and are not only pleased by being remembered through a traditional ritual but can influence the fortunes of the family and its members. The same understanding would apply to offerings made to deities in temples. But this understanding is reified by experiencing the actuality of these spirits when mediums are perceived to be embodied by these spirits.

Singular truth

Arising from monotheism is the understanding that there can only be a single Truth. Therefore, all other religious traditions are necessarily wrong, misguided, or incomplete. Other traditions or viewpoints, accordingly can be understood as a threat; hence, the justification for inquisitions and crusades. Polytheistic traditions are necessarily relativistic with regard to truth. Thus, in Chinese culture there is no potential tension between religious and other kinds of knowledge, such as scientific understandings, because truths are understood as multiple.

Life-cycle sacraments

Catholicism has seven sacraments necessary for salvation, including marriage (due to the doctrine of "Original Sin," sexual intercourse is sinful save when sanctified by the marriage ritual solely for the purpose of reproduction), which according to Church doctrine, symbolically represents the union of Jesus and the

Church. In other traditions, salvation, let alone salvation through sacraments, is uncommon, and the number of life-cycle rituals is far more limited and not sacramental. Traditionally in China, for example, marriage is a matter of relationships between families and the bringing of a new member into the patrilocal family, not to sanctify otherwise evil sexuality.

Focus on individuals

Although Christianity understands the Church to be the body of believers, the focus on individual salvation, along with a celibate priesthood, denigrates the family, an attitude found as early as the letters of Paul and the Gospels. Missionaries have informed Chinese that family rituals are the work of the Devil. This is contrary to all other major religions. Christianity focused on individual salvation because in its first generation it was expected that the world as we know it would come to an end. Because Roman religion included religion of family and state, Christianity's focus on the individual was perceived as a threat to the social order. Chinese culture is opposite to Christianity, and the focus is on the family, clan, and group, and individualism is secondary to family membership. Salvation as such is through the continuation of the family.

Creation myths

Creation myths are also part of the related traditions of Judaism and Islam, but most other religious traditions have instead origin myths, which may be of a clan, a culture, a city-state, etc. In these traditions, existence is a given prior to the particular origin narrative. It was often assumed by Western scholars that China had lost its origin myths (other than the popular Pangu version originally from India). What was not understood is that China has clan origin myths, as well as myths regarding the creation of humanity, rather than cosmic creation myths. Sky and Earth, as well as Yin and Yang, are dual creators. They arise from Nothingness becoming Somethingness, but they are not created from it. Moreover, this understanding is philosophical and experiential rather than mythic.

Immutable sacred written texts

Of the few religions outside of the Judeo-Christian-Islamic complex, or those influenced by them in this regard such as Sikhism, as in Buddhism, where there is a body of sacred texts, it is continuously augmented. The Vedas functions as a fixed, sacred oral text, but since Hinduism supplanted Vedism, it functions more as sacred utterances than as a text. The closest in China would be the Classics, but while they are highly respected, they are not revered as sacred.

Focus on abstruse ideology

Due to the development of theology in Christianity necessitated by ambiguous creeds and later influenced by the rebirth of Aristotelian logic in the Islamic universities which was passed on to Christian theologians by Jewish ones, who studied in the Muslim universities, other religions are taught in the West almost exclusively utilizing texts unknown to the vast majority of the studied religion's practitioners. Of course, this is also true of Christianity itself, especially premodern Catholicism, when all but a select few could read sacred texts. In China, the Classics primarily involve sociopolitical philosophy, and formal logic was laughed out of existence by such early texts as the *Zhuangzi*. In China, religious texts per se are pragmatic descriptions of ritual ranging from the three ritual texts in the Classics to Zhu Xi's *Family Rituals*.

Founder

There is a strong tendency to assume that all religions are founded. Thus, Jesus (or Paul) founds Christianity, Gautama founds Buddhism, Mohammed founds Islam, etc. But most religions are organic to and coexistent with specific cultures, and a consideration of a beginning is meaningless. Jesuit missionaries in China created the religion of Confucianism, assuming Kongzi to be the founder of religious rituals that had been in existence for well over a millennium prior to his life. Religious movements, however, do have beginnings and may, as Christianity, become major religious traditions. Chinese Religion is the oldest documented religion in the world, but its actual age would probably extend back to the beginning of agriculture, if not horticulture. Thus, to speak of a founder is nonsensical.

Ritual specialists as intermediaries between humans and the divine

The Catholic notion of the priest leads to the assumption that religious leaders in other traditions are understood to have similar sacred authority. This has led to many misunderstandings of the role of religious functionaries in other religions. In Chinese Religion, from a functional standpoint, the priests were the eldest males and females in the family and clan, and the chief priests of China in traditional times were the emperor and his consort (with ritual specialists to assist them), but none acted for the divine. Instead, the spirits of the family dead and divinities engaged directly with humans through entranced mediums, who have no priestly aura.

Professional religious competing or sharing power with secular authority

Christianity begins by denying the religious fundamentals of the Roman world (the family and the state as sacred) and was thus perceived as a threat to the common good and persecuted accordingly. This led the early Church to perceive itself as completely separate from the state. When the Roman Empire collapsed, the Church replaced the state, leading to a clash between state and religion when later European rulers sought independence from Church authority. (The eastern European and later English solution was for the secular ruler to become the head of the Church: caesaropapism.) This expectation has created grossly misleading understandings of other traditions. For example, so-called shamanistic cultures have been portrayed as having two authorities: a chief and a shaman, each vying for authority. Often these cultures are egalitarian and have no authorities. When they do, such as Manchurian culture, the shaman had no authority but served the political and clan authorities. Perhaps more important is the general assumption that religion can be separated out of culture, with the remainder termed "secular," and that there is a necessary tension between the two. In many traditions, as was the case in traditional China, the secular ruler was the chief priest of the society.

Religion is a male activity

Misogynist influences from Christian founders as Paul and Augustine, a male celibate priesthood, and the doctrine of original sin blaming Eve for the existence of sin combined to create the understanding that professional religious must be male. Indeed, early Western sociologists of religion, such as Durkheim, defined religion as solely within the male sociocultural sphere. As a counterexample, in patriarchal China, until a century ago, when the emperor performed religious rituals outside of the palace, his consort simultaneously and necessarily performed the same rituals inside the palace. In the early Chinese courts, the only exclusively religious functionaries were commonly women (see Paper 1997, 2016: Chapter 4).

Religious rituals take place in special sacred structures

Even though the earliest Christian rituals took place in synagogues, which are not sacred structures, there developed a tradition of churches, on the model of Roman temples and perhaps the Jerusalem temple, as the proper place for religious rituals. In the Hellenistic-Roman world, more rituals took place in the home than in temples, as is the case in many other parts of the world. Usually, such rituals are ignored in Western studies of religion, as rituals which do not take place in an assumed sacred structure are not considered religious rituals. In Taiwan, religions are categorized solely by buildings: temples for Chinese religions and churches for foreign religions. This is one of the major reasons that Chinese Religion is not recognized, for the majority of rituals take place in the home, and secondarily in clan temples, which are not sacred structures in themselves. American courts have denied protection for Native American sacred sites because they are usually not buildings.

Implications

After a century of so-called "humiliation," in the mid-twentieth century, Mainland China removed the remnants of colonial domination, including most Christian missionaries. China has since become an equal of all the previous colonizing nations and is on the way to becoming the most powerful nation on earth. In certain areas, as in economics and political structure, it has gone its own way, eventually to its advantage. But in other areas, such as political philosophy, it relies on the thinking arising from non-Chinese traditions, even where the non-Chinese way of thinking originated in China. With regard to religion, based on its past colonialist experience, the Chinese government does not allow religious institutions controlled or instigated by foreign nations. Yet China continues to understand and define religion from a colonialist perspective.

The Chinese government to date only recognizes religions recognized by the West, that is, religions which are perceived to accord with the Christian model. The only religion originating in China recognized is Daoism but from the skewed perspective of Christianity. Traditionally, most Daoists were hereditary, initiated part-time priests who served families and communities within Chinese Religion, as did Buddhist monks and nuns. Presently, the Daoism which is recognized in Mainland China is the aspect more closely modeled after Buddhism, itself of Indian origin, that is, the monastic mode of Daoism and those aspects which focus on individual salvation. Because Christian missionaries in general still consider Chinese Religion evil, it seems that China continues not to recognize its own religion. This amounts to a continuation of China being a colony of Christian nations, at least with regard to understanding religion.

More important, religion is the foundation and central core of cultures. Although some modern nations purport to be secular, alongside recognized religions they have created quasi-religions which have the same function. Thus, in the United States, Americanism, with its own mythos, rituals, and festivals, was created to allow for those of different religions to have a common ethos. During the Cultural Revolution in China, there was an attempt to replace the family in Chinese Religion with the Chinese people in general. This not only failed but led to a generation with little sense of moral values. Chinese Religion is now on the upswing on the mainland.

We must also recognize that the Chinese Communist Party, following Marxist-Leninist principles, considers membership in a religious institution as contrary to being a communist. Marx and Lenin, living in a Christian context, understood religion entirely on the Christian model. Marx opposed religion, specifically the religion preached to the proletariat, as an ideology used to persuade workers not to better their lot in this world but to await a better life after death. Hence, he understood that "Religion is the opium of the people" for the benefit of the factory owners in which the proletariat toiled in horrible conditions. Lenin perceived that the Russian Orthodox Church supported the aristocracy's maintenance of a feudal system with the peasants being serfs on the aristocratic estates. Thus for Lenin, religion also functioned to suppress the masses, and he consequently promoted atheism. Neither would necessarily condemn the liberal aspects of Western religion today and certainly were not specifically condemning such religious phenomenon as Chinese Religion.

If, in the Chinese context, *zongjiao* ("religion") is more specifically defined as "institutionalized religion," which is how Marx and Lenin understood religion, and another term is utilized to refer to non-institutionalized religion (called by some scholars "diffused religion"), that is, religion as conterminous with culture in general, the problem of not recognizing normative Chinese Religion as religion is resolved. Rather than refer to normative Chinese religious practices as *mixin* (superstition) or "folk religion" which denies the actuality of a tradition over five thousand years in age for both the elite and the masses, a term such a *wenli* meaning "ritual practices of the culture" or *Huarenjiao* "religion of the Chinese people" could be used. This would obviate the contradiction of supporting traditional Chinese ritual practices while not recognizing its existence. Many of the traditionally educated Chinese were atheists, in the sense of Marxist-Leninism, and yet supported offerings to the family and in state rituals. They perceived no contradiction between a disinclination to accept the divine powers of popular deities while reverencing the deceased of their clan, leading rituals to spiritually support the area under their authority, and ritually honoring literati heroes.

Part 2: Chinese Religion from a global perspective

Introduction

Western scholars who study Chinese Religion often assume they are doing comparative studies, but the time invested in mastering Chinese usually leaves little time for studying religions other than their specialty. Accordingly, not having a real comparative perspective, the tendency for many of these scholars is to understand Chinese Religion as unique.

My own research has had a different path. As I was working on defining and delineating Chinese Religion, I came to study other traditions as well. Due to several disparate factors which coincided, I began to become familiar with an ever increasing number of Native American traditions. At the same time, involvement in a team-taught course which included material on Condomblé led to my becoming interested in African-Brazilian and African-Caribbean religions and subsequently Central West African traditions, which are their roots.

At first I noticed little commonality between Native American traditions and China, as my experiences were in northern Ontario, although that later changed when I began to look at the horticultural and agricultural traditions to the south. But as soon as I looked at the Central West African traditions, I noticed strong resemblances with Chinese Religion and related concepts of sacred kingship. But how could that be, since diffusion was not a viable option? Later when studying Polynesian traditions, I again found the same religious construct. Colleagues pointed out to me similar patterns in ancient Greek and Roman traditions, and a graduate student of mine, with no prompting from me, found hints of it in early Israelite religion. Finally nearly twenty years ago, it all came together when at the Museum of Anatolian Civilizations in Ankara I learned that at Çatalhöyük, the earliest excavated major horticultural village, some dead adults were buried within the earthen platform beds, while others, especially children, were buried under the floors of dwellings.

The common construct which I consequently perceived I call "Familism" (*zuxianjiao* / in Japan: *jiajiao* / Zhu Xi : *jiali*), a term others have used to designate Chinese Religion alone, and a term now used in business studies with a different focus. In this book, I have been translating *xiao* as "Familism." Familism can be delineated by twelve common behavioral, social, and ideological characteristics, not all of which will be found in every instance:

1. nuclear and larger families exist within a clan structure;
2. individuals are psychologically as well as socially subordinate to family and clan;
3. on death one theoretically continues in the family as a spirit to assist the living;
4. most religious rituals are family, clan and, where relevant, state affairs;
5. homes and clan structures are the primary settings for most rituals;

6. senior members of the family and clan hold the primary priestly roles;
7. main ritual feature: living members of the family feeding the dead members;
8. the living can communicate with dead family members through spirit possession;
9. alcohol (or equivalent) is common in rituals and may facilitate spirit possession;
10. kingship falls on the most senior of the clan that has hegemony over other clans;
11. justification for kingship is the king being chief priest and parent of the nation;
12. anthropomorphic deities derive from the concept of spirits of the family dead.

The evolution of religion

In the last few years, the subject of the evolution of religion has again become popular. Although these new approaches seek to avoid the value-laden studies of the past, which understood a movement from primitive religion to the ultimate true religion of Christianity, they unconsciously continue to delineate religion from the Christian pattern and seek equivalents in the past. The theory which follows instead understands religion as arising from socioeconomic-cultural patterns contained within and determined by geographic, climate and related factors (religio-ecology) and does not require belief, anthropomorphic deities, ur-monotheism, etc.

The reason for the development of identical religious constructs in diverse regions can be understood from the standpoint of religio-ecology, particularly with the shift from semi-nomadic gathering-hunting to semi-sedentary horticulture-hunting. The construct becomes full-fledged with the development of agriculture and permanent habitations. Herding cultures tend to be anomalous in these regards. The development of horticulture initiated the most profound revolution in human history, with significant effects on religion, society, governance, culture, and the economy.

Prior to horticulture or other sedentary patterns (plentiful wild grains, abundant maritime resources), gathering-hunting communities generally consisted of small extended families with the concept of clan, when present, attenuated. In these traditions the dead are left behind, such as the scaffold burials on the North American Plains, as the community migrates from one source of subsistence to another in seasonal rounds, at least in those areas that have seasons. The dead are often feared. In some cultures, the name of the dead is never spoken. In some others, after the end of the mourning period, the dead are sent off with a feast and asked never to return. The effective spirit realm consists of weather and cosmic spirits, as well as the very animals and plants on which subsistence depends. The means of communicating with the numinous is through ecstatic states in which volition and memory are maintained—classic "shamanism"—different from classic spirit possession (see Chapter 5). Spirit possession is probably not possible with non-anthropomorphic spirits, as what would it mean for an other-than-human being to take control of a human? (Nonhuman spirits that are latter anthropomorphized can possess humans.) This religious construct appears to be ubiquitous in gathering-hunting cultures and can be understood as the first global religion in human history.

The bulk of subsistence came from gathering by women—plants, small mammals, fish, and birds. In the early stages of human development, males hunted mammals, mammals that are much larger and more dangerous than exist today—mammoths, mastodons, huge bisons, aurochs, and so forth. A single hunter cannot bring down such animals; rather it requires highly cooperative endeavors of a group, especially if serious injuries and deaths are to be kept to a minimum. To enable close cooperation and the fortitude to accomplish the task, rituals that enable group trances are required, such as circa-polar heat rituals ("sweat lodges") of considerable antiquity (see Paper 2007: 132–39). Later, as in Mesoamerica and the Amazonian forest, group trances were facilitated by the use of psychoactive substances (see Lamb 1974).

A revolution occurs with the inception of horticulture. The gathering-hunting pattern is maintained in that females shift from gathering to gardening and males continue to hunt. The sedentary residential pattern, however, means that humans can live to a very old age and become a repository of cultural knowledge and history. As the dead are disposed of in the vicinity of the dwellings, the dead remain with the living and can continue to advise them. The obvious reason for burying the adult dead within the sleeping platforms at Çatalhöyük in Anatolia is so that the living members of the family can communicate with the dead members through dreams. This may have been the original impetus for spirit possession.

The excavations at Çatalhöyük also indicate the development of clan organization and structures for clan religious rituals. The dead were not evenly distributed among the homes but tended to be concentrated in a home around which other homes without burials were clustered. Certainly, this strongly suggests a clan socio-religious structure, as well as selected homes serving as ritual centers for the clan as a whole.

In horticulture-hunting traditions (or the northwest coastal North American and mid-west coastal South American village traditions with their abundant maritime resources), clans become more important than nuclear families, with multiple families often living in clan longhouses. The head of the clan takes on a more commanding leadership role than in the volunteerism of gathering-hunting situations. More importantly, the head of the clan becomes the symbol of the clan itself. This role continues after death, so that dead "clan mothers" or dead clan chieftains and their spouses become more important spirits than those of ordinary members of the clan.

Knowledge too expands. Male hunters still need their specialized knowledge, but the gathering knowledge of females expands to incorporate the knowledge that horticulture requires. With the greater knowledge of women and with women's "ownership" of the gardens, along with the clan longhouses, these cultures are generally matrilocal, matrilineal, and matrifocal rather than fully egalitarian as before.

Religion also changes radically. Seasonal rituals become more important, outside of the equatorial regions, as planting and harvesting fertility rituals are celebrated. The spirit realm now includes the dead of the clan and the controlling spirits of the garden. The very act of preparing gardens and planting leads to an understanding of limited control over subsistence. This in turn leads to a notion of controlling subsistence spirits, such as the Mother of the Garden, rather than the individual spirits in the gathering-hunting situation. (A similar transformation takes place in the shift from hunting to herding, for example, the Reindeer Mother in north-central Siberia.)

Gardening leads to the fermentation of starches or sugary fruits to provide alcohol for ritual group inebriation. Alternately, kava was raised on the Pacific islands, chocolate was farmed in Mesoamerica, coca was grown in the Andes, tobacco was planted throughout much of the Americas, and so forth. Such inebriation-stimulated trances promoted an intimate interaction between the living and the dead, and in some cultures, as in early Chinese elite culture, facilitated some becoming possessed by the dead of the clan. Thus, the dead, and later deities, could now be directly spoken to and touched.

The development of agriculture led to further major changes in human culture although not as radical as the earlier transformation. Settlements became even more permanent as humans learned to fertilize and irrigate the agricultural fields. Male farming shifted the economic focus from females to males, and surplus productivity allowed for the development of non-subsistence occupations and thus class distinctions. The first non-productive class was of warriors who used non-hunting weapons, such as chariots, that required long-term specialist training and led to a male-dominated society as the leading warrior, usually a male, became a king. The need to protect the surplus productivity was extended to warfare against other agricultural communities to create kingdoms. The patrifocal nature of kingdoms led to patriarchy in some but not all such cultures.

The king and the later expanded role of emperor continued the function of the superior clan chieftain as political head, symbol of the group and chief priest. The concept of family and clan is enlarged to include kingdom and empire. The emperor and his consort become the ultimate parents. Rituals became more complex and state rituals developed as expanded clan rituals. Upon death, the former king or emperor became an even more powerful clan spirit, although not a deity. Anthropomorphic deities were non-family dead human spirits with powers capable of benefiting humans in general and also able to possess mediums in order to interact with the human realm.

Familism

An excellent, concise statement of the understanding of ancestral spirits from within one of these traditions can be found in the words of a female Hawaiian elder when asked to explain the meaning of *aum~kua*, meaning "ancestral spirits" but not "deities," which are termed *akua* (her English-language statement is somewhat misleading in this regard, for if stated in Polynesian *aum~kua* would not be conflated with *akua*):

> In *Po* [the infinite, timeless spirit realm] there dwell our ancestors, transfigured into gods. They are forever god-spirits, possessing the strange and awesome powers of gods. Yet they are forever our relatives, having for us the loving concern a mother feels for her infant, or a grandfather for his first-born grandson. As gods and relatives in one, they give us strength when we are weak, warning when danger threatens, guidance in our bewilderment, inspiration in our arts. They are equally our judges, hearing our words and watching our actions, reprimanding us for error, and punishing us for blatant offense. For these are our godly ancestors. These are our spiritual parents. These are our *aum~kua*.
>
> You and I, when our time has come, shall plunge from our *leina* [special seaside cliff from which the spirit on death plunges into *Po*] into *Po*. If our lives have been worthy, our *aum~kua* will be waiting to welcome us. Then we too shall inhabit the eternal realm of the ancestor spirits. We in our time shall become *aum~kua* to our descendants even yet unborn. (Pukui 1972: 35)

When I read this passage, without the Polynesian words, at a conference of specialists on living Chinese Religion, everyone without exception assumed I was presenting a statement from a Chinese informant.

This religious pattern, which can be termed "Familism," can be found in East Asia (China, Korea, Japan and Vietnam), sub-Saharan African traditions, Melanesia, Micronesia, Polynesia, early Israelite religion, classical Greek and Roman religion, in some Native American agricultural traditions (e.g., western South America), and undoubtedly in others with which I am unfamiliar. The interrelated monotheistic traditions, particularly Christianity, moved away from Familism to embrace its ideological opposite: individual salvation. Anti-family statements can be found as early as the letters of Paul and the words attributed to Jesus in the Gospels. Similarly, Buddhism earlier began with individuals seeking release from the cycle of existence who rejected their own families. Buddhist monasticism, as early Chinese critics readily pointed out, denied the very basis of Chinese Religion and society, until it became Sinicized.

If this pattern is as common as I am arguing, how come it has not been previously acknowledged? Since religious studies arose in Christian culture, Christianity became the model for normative religion as discussed in Part I, and Familism meets none of the resultant expectations. First, Christianity is institutional, the institution called the Church. Familism is non-institutional: there is no clergy save for assisting ritual specialists under certain circumstances. Second, Christian rituals primarily take place in special buildings, Churches, that are normally open to all adherents. In Familism, the primary rituals take place in the home or in clan temples that are not open to the public; hence, they remain unseen to outsiders. Third, Christianity focuses on a single deity in three aspects who is omniscient and omnipotent. In Familism, rituals are oriented toward the family or clan itself with a focus on the deceased of the family.

From the common Western perspective, it is difficult to understand how religion can be a matter of family, since it is understood that religion is about the belief in God or divinities. Furthermore, it is assumed that all cultures value families as important to the social order. But the difference is in the degree of valuation. In Christian cultures, the family is not revered, rituals are not directed toward the family, and the continuation of the person after death is understood to be a matter of individual salvation, not a matter of integration into the spiritual dimension of the family. Thus, those in the West are culturally and religiously programmed not to recognize Familism.

Moreover, the West is antagonistic to Familism, as it runs counter to contemporary Western values. The Universal Declaration of Human Rights of the United Nations is entirely about the rights of individuals, separate from family, and where family is mentioned, it is only the nuclear family which is meant. Indeed the Declaration if actually carried out would wrest the individual from being integral to family, and thus is inimical to the social structure and philosophy of such recent enemies at that time it was promulgated as Japan. It is a boon to Christian missionaries, for if actually enforced, it would destroy family religion, encouraging only the religions of individual salvation.

Let me provide a concrete example of the difference between a culture which primarily values individualism and one which primarily values family. In the mid-1960s, while engaged in the first international kendo tournament being held in Taiwan, I became acquainted with a Japanese businessman and kendo practitioner who became my sponsor when I later further studied kendo in Japan. One day he invited me to practice at his *dojo* (practice hall) in Osaka and afterward took me to a private bathhouse and then dinner at his private club. He controlled a family-owned multimillion dollar business; but it was his family members, not he himself, who were very rich and powerful. At dinner, he asked how I was able to get my family to approve my travels and was amazed when I told him that I never sought their permission. In contrast to me, he was bound by family obligations and could not act independently.

A further answer to the question "If Familism is so obvious, why has it not been more recognized?" lies in the nature of religious studies, which developed in Europe far earlier than in North America. The late-nineteenth-century theorists were stuck in the then anthropological ideology of racism and in its corollary ideological context justifying European colonialism. Accordingly, it was assumed that Greco-Roman civilization was superior to Chinese civilization, and both were far superior to sub-Saharan African civilizations, which must, due to dark skin color, be primitive. A contrary approach was made by the forerunners of religio-ecology, such as Pettazoni and latter Hultkrantz, but they tended toward simplistic studies linking early economic patterns to theology. Others, such as Eliade, created patterns from the Christian experience in which to slot other religious traditions, often forcibly.

Comparative perspectives

Most religionists tend to focus on studying particular traditions in depth, taking time to master the requisite languages. Consequently, they tend to view their subject of study as cultural isolates, being unique instances of religion. The exceptions are scholars of Christianity, who often assume that their subject matter is a superior version of a common form of religion, other religions missing essential elements that can only be supplied by Christianity.

Perhaps my own difference in this regard is that I began a study of comparative religious studies methodologies only after becoming immersed in Chinese language and culture and thus approached the enterprise from a Chinese perspective rather than a Western one. Also, when I first had the opportunity to live in Chinese culture in Taiwan in my sixth year of graduate studies, after being there but a few days, I was most fortunate in being invited by a fellow student to a lunar bimonthly *baibai* (ritual offering). This was at the home of a family friend. Chinese tend not to invite any but the most intimate of friends to their homes, using restaurants in urban areas for social gatherings. Thus, at the very beginning of my directly experiencing Chinese culture, I was able to observe the basic ritual of Familism normally hidden behind residential walls. That experience became the foundation of my study of Chinese culture and religion.

Later, after becoming engrossed in the Native American Anishnabe religion, I added that to my perspectives. Especially important was through intense participation to be able to internalize an understanding of polytheism. By the time I was looking at African and Polynesian traditions, I was already psychologically multicultural, imbued with Jewish-Western, Chinese and northern Native American essential understandings.

From these multiple perspectives, I perceived that all cultures arose from a single commonality—the human being—and that humans are all essentially the same. Such a viewpoint accepts that cultures became increasingly complex but that humans themselves have not changed for at least the last fifty thousand years, and probably the last two hundred thousand years, as has been recently been borne out by the earliest upper Paleolithic finds, and that most cultures are no better than any other, each being a response to its ecological situation. The same is the case for religion, each a product of a particular religio-ecology but created by humans, all similar to each other.

A new approach to the study of religion

This approach reverses the usual way of looking at religion. Instead of looking at a religion as a unique complex, we can look at most religions as variations on a common theme, not too different from musical compositions that are variations on a theme. Hence, if we look at Chinese Religion, for example, from this perspective, we would not consider the major structure and rituals unique but perceive that they are one with this horticultural-agricultural religious complex. What we can then examine are those aspects that are different from others, those aspects not to be found in other traditions, save those shared with other East Asian cultures due to diffusion. Thus, as examples, the way other religions such as Buddhism have been Sinicized and integrated or how individual religious concerns have been dealt with are of considerable interest. For example, Daoism as an adjunct institutionalized religion initially focused on individual transformation. But when Daoism integrated with normative Chinese Religion, it became in effect, aside from the monastic stream modeled on Buddhism, rent-a-ritualist family corporations. Traditionally, those called Daoists in China, aside from the monastic variant, are initiated members of a hereditary priestly lineage, who work as part-time ritual specialists when hired to conduct funerals or village renewal rituals.

Understanding Chinese Religion from this perspective explains how Familism provided an ideological basis for unifying the first functional Chinese empire. As Asoka consolidated the Maurya Empire in India by promoting Buddhism and Constantine attempted to consolidate a reunited Roman Empire with Christianity, so the government of the Han Empire unified a hitherto fragmented semi-feudal sociopolitical situation by expanding Familism to include the state through expanding the meaning of *xiao* (Familism) to include the emperor as on a par with one's father and mother.

Of interest too is how Chinese Religion, given its religio-ecological basis, accords with modernity, such as the industrial and post-industrial milieus and the shift away from imperial government. For example, both on the Chinese mainland and in Taiwan, heads of state or their delegates are now starting to take on the nation-wide parental-priestly roles of the past a full century after the collapse of the imperial regime. Such developments indicate how strong the religious roots are. Perhaps most telling in this regard was when several decades ago, the deceased Mao Tse-tung, the foremost Chinese communist and Marxist-Leninist atheist, became the new deity of capitalistic wealth (he has since, I have been recently informed, become a protecting deity as well).

This approach to the study of religion reverses even the usual approach to the study of the monotheistic traditions. Rather than seeing them as the norm, they can be viewed as a radical change from this second major global religion. While Judaism and Islam have only moved partially from this core, with family remaining important and an understanding of the entire religious community as an enormous clan, Christianity in its inception seems to have been anti-family, with a focus on individual salvation. Thus, until it became the dominant religion, Christianity was perceived by the larger culture as a threat to the social order. Even today, the heads of the Roman Catholic and of the various Orthodox Christian traditions are, at least theoretically, celibate. Tension between religion and state remained throughout Christian history, save when the two coincided, with the head of the state and of the state religion being one and the same, as in Orthodox Christianity and the Church of England.

To the contrary, Buddhism too began with a focus on individual salvation and a disinterest in family—we must keep in mind that Gautama left his wife and children and his duties to his parents and state in order to seek his own salvation. But as Buddhism became a religion with a community beyond those who also left family, it slowly changed toward concern for the larger community. With the development of Mahayana, the situation was reversed and individual salvation was rejected as selfish and the goal was salvation of all living beings simultaneously, a notion even larger than humanity itself. Thus, only the Mahayana modes of Buddhism were able to successfully integrate into and merge with the religions of Central and East Asia.

In contrast, save in Korea, Christianity has been remarkably unsuccessful in East Asia, in large part because of the attitude toward this common notion of family. In Central Africa, Christianity has been relatively successful but only after European countries destroyed traditional African governments and social structure through colonialism, and replaced local languages with European ones among the elite.

In French-controlled Polynesia, the Catholic Church forcibly destroyed the indigenous religion; the French government destroyed the traditional government; and the modern economy has wiped out the colonial imposed economy which replaced the traditional one. Only in Hawaii and New Zealand did Polynesian religion survive underground and is now very slowly rising in a modern context as indigenous peoples there gain a modicum of behavioral freedom.

Regarding Mesoamerica and South America, the familial religious complex continues within a Christian overlay in Yucatan after an accord was reached following Mayan revolts from the mid-nineteenth through the early twentieth centuries. Contrastingly, in Chiapas, the struggle continues. The election of an indigenous president in Ecuador has seen a public resurgence of Andean rituals. In North America, the Pueblo cultures reached an accord allowing for parallel religions following a successful revolt against the Spanish in the late seventeenth century, and the Hopi continued their traditional religion partially due to inaccessibility. The Hopi have been successful in controlling religious tourism, while the Huichol further south, who maintained their traditions by fleeing to the mountains and then killing missionaries who followed them, have seen the commercialization of their religion due to this type of tourism. These are but a few examples of how Familism has been impinged upon by religions that do not focus on family.

Thus, the basic religious substrate of Familism is largely unrecognized in religious studies because it is contrary to Western understandings. Where it continued, the Christian West has set about to deliberately destroy it through the missionary-colonial enterprise or inadvertently by its contemporary touristic variant. Hence, the question remains as to whether religious studies will ever move from considering the Christian model to be normative and thus allow for genuinely comparative studies.

A Chinese approach to studying religion

With regard to Chinese culture, imagine the difference if religious studies scholars in China and Taiwan understood Chinese Religion to be the major example of a global religious complex with a ten-thousand-year history. Chinese Religion then would not be negatively perceived from a Christian colonial perspective but as a religion with a far longer history and far greater connections to other cultures than the Western religions.

Besides, the study of religion did not begin with Christian missionaries in the sixteenth century. Early Greek and Roman scholars were interested in studying religion, and Chinese scholars were the first to study religion from what is now considered a social science perspective. Around 2,400 years ago, Xunzi studied ritual from the perspective of its social role and ritual studies continued in China to the present. Chinese scholars should be aware of other cultures' approach to the study of religion, but for the roots of religious studies, they need go no further than their own scholarly traditions.

The word religion, it is generally albeit not universally agreed, derives from Roman times with the Latin word *religāre*, meaning "to bind." It was used in medieval Christianity to apply to monks who are bound to their order by a vow of obedience. Thus, the explicit Christian use of the term is in accord with Xunzi's understanding of *li*, "ritual." It is rituals that bind individuals to family and bind the family together; secondarily, rituals bind families to the larger sociocultural matrix; and finally, rituals derived from the family rituals bind the state or, in modern terms, the nation together.

After Xunzi's time, as Buddhism and Daoism became part of the Chinese cultural matrix, aside from the transformative rituals for individuals, they provided additional, adjunct family and community rituals, along with temple worship. Since the Song dynasty, Chinese deities are understood as parallel to the family and clan spirits, being dead humans who can assist living humans of all clans. This concept may have been stimulated by the transformation of Bodhisattvas into deities, such as Guanyin. Chinese Islam and Judaism (see Chapter 9) also assimilated to the religion of family, adding further rituals to the ones they brought with them to China. When Catholic Christianity was first introduced by Jesuits, they promulgated a Christianity that also served in conjunction with the family and state rituals. Although this approach was later repudiated by the Vatican, it was brought back with Vatican II in the 1960s.

Thus, normative Chinese Religion, however it is named, has been the only practice and ideology that has bound together the enormous, relatively speaking, geographical extent and population of China. Moreover, Chinese Religion, rather than being distinctly different from socialism, posits socioeconomic understandings—including a relatively equitable distribution of economic resources—that have been part and parcel of Chinese *rujia* thinking since at least the time of the writing of the *Mengzi*, some 2,400 years ago.

Conclusion

Understanding their own religion, the basis of their culture and social structure, from a foreign, often negative, Christian perspective, has led modern Chinese governments to marginalize if not ignore it. This attitude continues, even though government officials in both Taiwan and China take part in public religious rituals. This lack of recognition encourages Chinese scholars in religious studies to study non-Chinese religions, as well as Buddhism and Daoism, but to disregard Chinese Religion itself. Moreover, this lack of recognition of Chinese Religion in China supports Western governments' tendency to not recognize Chinese Religion which has deleterious effects on their own constituents of Chinese background.

Understanding religion based on the Christian model, which lacks general applicability, however, is not necessary. Other models of religious modalities, such as Familism, are available which allows for a comparative understanding of Chinese Religion. Familism places Chinese Religion within a global construct which arose over ten thousand years ago with the inception of horticulture and continues in the present to varying degrees in religions other than Christianity. There is now a growing interest among the younger generation of Chinese scholars in their own traditions; hence, in the future we can expect a Chinese approach to the study of religion in China, which should greatly enhance our understanding.

4

The Theology Implicit in the Early Confucian Tradition: The Fundamental Understanding of the Meaning of Life in Chinese Culture

Introduction

"Theology," literally "the study of male deities," is generally understood to mean the study of deities or God, primarily in the Christian sense. But there is a long history of understanding the term more generally, even within the Christian tradition. Boethius (2004), writing in the early sixth century, used the term for a subdivision of philosophy that studies motionless, incorporeal reality: "Theology deals with the abstract, which lacks motion and is separable" (Evans 1980: 31–2). Here, in this chapter, "theology" is used broadly to refer to how the numinous is understood and approached. Chinese theology is a version of Familism that can be found in virtually all horticultural and agricultural societies, and their extension into industrial and post-industrial cultures that have not been transformed by universal religions of individual salvation, such as Christianity. In these societies, religion and culture are synonymous, and the family in and of itself is the primary numinous. Individuals understand themselves first and foremost as members of social groups. Society is understood to be more important than the individual, opposite to the contemporary Western 'human rights' stance, which gives precedence to the rights of the individual over that of society.

Much has been written on Chinese deities, but little by Sinologists grounded in comparative religion. Chinese scholars tend to write on the topic from the purview of mythological studies and folkloristics (e.g., Ke 1993, Cheng 1995, Yang and An 2005). There have been a number of excellent studies of recipients of early Chinese ritual offerings by philologists and historians (e.g., Keightly 1978). Historians have written on Chinese deities in particular periods (e.g., Hansen

1990). Studies have also been written reflecting Christian rather than Chinese viewpoints regarding early Chinese theology, many finding a monotheistic to semi-monotheistic High God with the characteristics applied to God by those imbued with a literal reading of the Hebrew Bible (see "Relevant Cognitive and Neurological Studies" in Chapter 2). This study will argue against this last understanding by examining from the standpoint of comparative theology the most important early Chinese text containing discussions regarding theology, a text that is the foundation of the dominant Chinese ideology until the early twentieth century. The theology reflected in this text, the *Lunyu (Analects)* of Kongzi (Confucius), remains the primary religious understanding in Chinese culture today.

Before proceeding, it is necessary to unpack a problematic term in this chapter's title: "Confucian," which is used in the title because it is very familiar to Western readers. The term, however, has no early Chinese equivalent. "Confucianism," when referring to a religion, was first used by Jesuit missionaries at the end of the sixteenth century in order to divide Chinese Religion (*huaren jiao*) into a triune set of separate religions: Confucianism, Daoism, and Buddhism (see Chapter 2).

The term "Confucianism," when referring to philosophy, is used to translate the Chinese term *rujia* (scholarly tradition), the ever-evolving ideological basis of traditional Chinese government. It is called Confucianism, as Islam was once called Mohammedanism, due to the assumption that all religions and ideologies must be named after a presumed founder. Kongzi ("Master Kong," 551–479 BCE, sometimes with an added honorific: Kongfuzi, Latinized as Confucius), is understood in China as the First Teacher. Indeed, he is the first professional teacher in recorded history. He made his living as a teacher because he could not obtain an important government position, and he considered his life a failure for that reason. He taught potential officials, emphasizing ethics and ritual, and some of his students did obtain high offices. Thus, he is the founder of a theoretically principled government composed of educated bureaucrats chosen for ability instead of officials inheriting their positions as before. He considered himself not an innovator but a transmitter of the past; thus, in his own mind, he was not a founder of anything.

Although we have nothing that Kongzi actually wrote, after his death his students began to recollect in writing what they remembered of his teachings. These brief statements and anecdotes were collected into a work called the *Lunyu* (*Analects*), to which additions were made over the following several centuries (which are additions is controversial). It is this work on which the theological analysis in this study will be based.

None of the works earlier than most of the *Lunyu* provide an understanding of commonplace early elite Chinese theology. The excavated written material from before three thousand years ago, when the Zhou dynasty replaced the Shang, consists of very brief texts written on prognostication material. While the queries are directed toward the numinous, how the numinous was understood is somewhat opaque and remains controversial. It is certain though that the numinous does refer to ancestral spirits in varying ways. The earliest extant book, the *Yi (Changes)*, is a prognostication manual that is still in use today. It does not query numinous entities but seeks to indicate the direction in which the cosmos and its aspects are proceeding so that we can adapt our behavior to it in order to be successful. Centuries after it was written, appendixes were added to the *Yi* to convert the work to a philosophical treatise.

The other extant early books are collected historical documents and odes, some sung at the ancestral offering ritual, which inform us about the rituals of the time. In essence, these are the same rituals found in Chinese culture today. Texts on ritual developed before and during the time of Kongzi were finalized several centuries after he lived. Kongzi focused on ritual in his teaching and ethics. Hence, the *Lunyu* is the first Chinese work to reflect but not intentionally discuss the general theological understanding underpinning these rituals in early Chinese culture.

Kongzi was hardly a theologian; indeed, he was known to avoid speaking about the spirit realm—we shall return to this point later. There are but a few handfuls of references to spirits in the text. But these references, and the use of other related terms, inform us of the basis of their system of ethics and, of foremost importance, ritual—indeed, of how they understood existence and the meaning of life and death. Hence, the theology reflected in the *Lunyu* is implicit rather than explicit.

China did have a rich mythic lore replete with powerful deities, some half-human, as well as demons, and so forth, but the intelligentsia tended not to discuss this topic and no mention will be found in the *Analects*. Also, China at the time of Kongzi was not a unified culture. Only several centuries later, with the first successful empire, the Han dynasty, do we find cultural and religious homogenization and writings on these topics. After this time, Mahayana Buddhism slowly starts to have its impact on Chinese Religion and in turn Chinese Religion begins to transform Buddhism in China. Simultaneously, Daoism, as institutionalized sects adjunct to Chinese Religion, begins to develop. By a thousand years ago, there were a number of beneficent spirits who are non-family dead, perhaps modeled on the Bodhisattva, a deceased human who has postponed entering Nirvana to assist living people. These developments function as adjuncts to Chinese Religion. But all this takes place long after the discourses to be found in the *Analects*.

Also not to be found in the *Analects* is the understanding of the numinous that arises from the mystic experience—that at the heart of all that exists is nothingness. This appears a century after Kongzi in the early strata of the *Zhuangzi* and later became the metaphysical foundation of Chinese philosophy (see Paper 2004: 89–101). It is relatable to the understanding of God and the Godhead to be found in Meister Eckhardt's writings as a Western example. What the *Analects* does provide is an understanding of the numinous that continues to the present in China.

This chapter centers on three questions. First, was Kongzi, as is often averred, agnostic? For if he was, then statements regarding the numinous in the *Lunyu* would be of little consequence. Second, did Kongzi have an understanding of a monotheistic deity or a "High God," as is often posited? Third, if not, then how was the numinous understood and engaged?

Early Chinese Religion

Early Chinese Religion—known from tomb furnishings, prognostication texts, ritual odes and later extensive writings on the rituals—is an example of Familism, as discussed in Chapters 1 and 3. To summarize, in Chinese Religion, the primary numinous is the family in and of itself, the family understood as the nuclear family on the micro level and the extended clan on the macro level. After the creation of the first stable Chinese empire, the Han, over two thousand years ago, the notion of family was extended in political thought to a third level, encompassing all of China, indeed the whole world, with the emperor and his consort being the Father and Mother of all people, and both serving as the chief priests of the world. Only they on behalf of all people have the prerogative to make formal offerings to the progenitor couple of all that exists—Sky-Earth (*Tiandi*)—as well as the founding ancestors of the ruling clan.

The family was understood to exist both horizontally and vertically in time. On the one hand, it included all those of the same surname—and there are relatively few surnames for all of the Chinese population—and on the other hand, it includes those of the past, present, and future. It is the relationship of the ruling clan to their powerful ancestors that is the theoretical basis of their political power. The first act of a clan on conquering a ruling clan was to pull down the defeated clan's ancestral temple and build a new one of their own.

These relationships were based on reciprocity. As the parents conceive, birth and nurture children, so children when grown nurture their aged parents, and when the parents die, continue to nurture them by ritually offering food and drink, which is then enjoyed by the celebrants as a family banquet when the honored guests, the spirits of the dead, are satiated. As the ancestors are cared for, so the living can expect the dead to help the living in turn. Individuals do not comprehend themselves as do individuals in traditions of individual salvation, because salvation for individuals lies in the continuity of the family itself—a contemporary example will be presented near the end of this chapter. The family is foremost in mind rather than one's individual self, and individuals strive to both continue the family line and enhance its viability and vitality as the religious imperative.

For the aristocratic clans, the offering to the family and clan dead was an elaborate ritual involving vessels that were the richest and most technologically advanced that could be created—the well-known bronze ritual vessels—with a small orchestra, dancers, and orations. The priest, the one officially making the offering, was the eldest son or daughter-in-law of the deceased, depending on the gender of the primary recipient in the patrilineage.

The second most important person in the ritual was the Incorporator of the Dead (*shi*, literally, "corpse"—strangely called in other translations the Impersonator of the Dead) who is usually the grandson or granddaughter-in-law of the offering recipient. The Incorporator of the Dead, chosen by prognostication, fasts and meditates on the dead recipient for a number of days, is escorted to the clan temple as if he or she were the deceased, drinks nine cups of wine during the ritual and is then possessed by the spirit of the deceased. This medium for the deceased then eats and drinks from the offering until the orator announces, "The spirits are drunk," at which point the spirits leave as the Incorporator of the Dead is escorted from the temple. The food and drink are then transferred from the clan temple to a hall, where the living attendees enjoy the feast.

This ritual became the model for all of the relationships of the aristocracy which were highly ritualized. And this ritual in reduced form continues among Chinese families, and in full mode in Taipei at an annual state-sponsored offering ritual to the literati heroes of the past, especially Kongzi. At the full and new moons each month, a feast is laid out before the ancestral tablets on the family altar. After prognostication indicates that the spirits had their fill of the spiritual aspect of the offering, the food is moved to the dining table and eaten by the family. On special occasions the food will be brought first to the clan temple for an initial offering there. If the family has difficulties, they may ask a medium to be embodied by a deceased member of the family so they can consult with her or him. Other rituals to nature spirits, to agricultural fertility and mercantile spirits, to martial and civil authority spirits by government officials, to Buddhist Bodhisattvas and Daoist deities, etc., are modeled on the family offering ritual.

Statements in the Lunyu *relevant to theology*

The terms in the *Lunyu* that denote the numinous are "*"shen"* and "Tian." *Shen* has been traditionally translated as "God" or "gods," "deities," "spirits" and "soul." Depending on context, it can mean any of these, save the first. For this reason, the term in this chapter will not be translated, allowing the meaning to depend on its specific import in a particular passage.

Tian has often been understood by many but far from all Western scholars to be an anthropomorphic monotheistic deity. An excellent discussion of the history of this understanding, as well as the question as to whether Confucianism is a religion, can be found in a relatively recent article by Huang (2007), and there is no need to repeat her analysis here. One of the most important contemporary proponents of this view is Edward Slingerland:

> The religious worldview of the Zhou borrowed heavily from the dynasty they replaced. . . . [They adopted] the Shang god, the Lord on High [Shangdi], who was conflated with and eventually replaced by their own tribal god, *tian*. . . . "Heaven" is a fairly good rendering of *tian*, as long as the reader keeps in mind that "Heaven" refers to an anthropomorphic figure—someone who can be communicated with, angered or pleased—rather than a physical place. (Confucius 2003: xviii)

My own understanding of Shangdi radically differs. The Shang rulers made ancestral offerings to Shangdi. I accept the understanding that at that time *di* ("power") was the aggregate of ancestral spirits of the aristocratic clans. Hence, when the ritual offering was not to a particular ancestor, then it was to all the ancestors or Di. Shangdi ("Superior Power") was sometimes used to denote the ancestral spirits of the ruling or superior clan. Slingerland does note that "the Lord on High [Shangdi] was the blood ancestor of the Shang royal line"

(Confucius 2003: xix), but there is no logical necessity to understand the term to be singular—that is, referring to a monotheistic deity—rather than a collective. In the nineteenth century, Protestant missionaries chose to use Shangdi to translate God into Chinese. From a perverse circular logic, the Christian meaning is often read back into the distant past to understand Shangdi to be a singular monotheistic deity from a Protestant perspective. Earlier, Catholic missionaries used the term *tianzhu* (Ruler of Tian) as their translation for God, thus Tian in the distant past is similarly understood to mean a monotheistic, anthropomorphic deity.

Tian can variously mean simply the sky above us, as well as the clouds and so forth that exist in the sky; the progenitor of all that exists in the compound *Tiandi* (Sky-Earth—sometimes the compound is represented by *Tian* alone); prognosis or fate, especially in the term *Tianming*, meaning the star-pattern, astrology-astronomy being an essential aspect of early Chinese government; and, most importantly for this chapter, the aggregate of the deceased important persons—this includes both the most important deceased rulers of the ruling clan and/or (depending on context) the mythic sage-rulers and culture heroes. Tian in the latter sense represents the souls of the great that rise to Sky, in contrast to the souls that descend to Earth, China having an understanding of at least two souls in each human. Thus to today, offerings are made to the soul below in the earth at the grave or tomb and above to the soul in the sky at the name plaque on the family altar or in the clan temple.

The *Lunyu* is certainly not a work on theology. Indeed, in the work it is noted that among the topics that Kongzi did not discuss was *shen* (Book 7, Section 21), although the term is mentioned in nine places and implied in seven more. Rather, the work centers on education, ethics, and political philosophy. The focus of education is ritual. Ethics is based on *xiao* (Familism), a concept which puts at the forefront rituals directed toward the dead of the family. Political philosophy revolves around proper ritual behavior. The political rituals both subsume and are based on the rituals to the dead of the family. The term for the dead of the family is *shen*, and Tian in this context means the aggregate of the dead of the clan. Hence, the background understanding of *shen* and Tian expressed in the *Lunyu* connotes the commonly understood theology of the Chinese elite two-and-a-half millennia in the past. This is an understanding that is the essence of Chinese Religion, given the continuity of this ritual in most details from the distant past, long before the writing of the *Lunyu*, to the present.

The above-mentioned statement regarding Kongzi's disinclination to discuss *shen*, when combined with the following statement has been interpreted by a number of Western scholars that Kongzi was agnostic regarding *shen*, if not dismissive of their reality: "Make offerings to shen with the understanding that the *shen* are actually present" (3,12). (Translations are my own; other excellent translations are D. C. Lau 1979 and Ames and Rosemont Jr. 1998.) In the first half of the twentieth century, Western scholars writing on Kongzi assumed their Humanist sympathies were also the understanding of a person they admired. What this passage actually expresses in the context of other statements on ritual is that when one takes part in an offering ritual, sincerity is of utmost importance.

Sincerity was essential because *xiao* was stated by Kongzi to be the pinnacle of ethical behavior. When asked what that meant, Kongzi said, "When alive serve [parents] according to the proper rituals; when dead, bury them with the proper rituals and make offerings to [their *shen*] with the proper rituals" (2,6). Here *shen* is implied but not expressly stated. In this regard, the importance of the offering rituals to the family dead can be seen in the following: when praising the mythic sage-king Yu, Kongzi said, "Yu was faultless. He ate and drank simply yet was generous in his offerings to his family spirits (*gueishen*)" (8,21). *Gueishen* is a rare compound expression (which later disappeared) in early Chinese that fuses *guei* (ghost) with *shen* (spirit). In replying to a question as to how one should serve the spirits of the deceased (*gueishen*), Kongzi replies: "Just as if one does not understand life, one cannot understand death, so if one is yet incapable of serving the living, one is incapable of serving *shen*" (11,12). Nothing is more important than the offering rituals to the family and clan dead.

On the other hand, "To make offerings to the deceased spirits (*guei*) that are not one's own [i.e., other families' *shen*] is the height of insincerity" (2,24). The ritual offerings are to family *shen* by their descendants only, although rulers would be assisted by ritual specialists when carrying out their grand rituals. Hence, "Being respectful to the deceased spirits (*gueishen*) of other families while not approaching them is being wise" (6,22). It is commonly understood today that making offerings to the *shen* of other families is both inappropriate and dangerous. When such rituals became state rituals, the family connection was not lost. Nowadays, in Taipei at the annual offering to Kongzi at the Temple to the First Teacher (also called the Literary/Culture Temple [*wenmiao*] traditionally to be found in all administrative centers), the state-supported offering is made by an assumed descendant of Kongzi (one whose family name is Kong) who is centrally present, although all of the ritual movements are actually carried out by university teachers and students acting as ritual assistants.

Aside from the mentioning of family *shen*, there are also references to other types of *shen* in the *Lunyu*. For example, on the occasion of Kongzi being ill, his disciple requests a favorable outcome from the realm of nature spirits: "sky and earth *shen*" (7,35). In the work there is mention of offerings to Mount Tai discussed in Chapter 1 (the premier sacred site in northeastern China), meaning the *shen* of Mount Tai (3,6); the Stove (or Hearth) *shen* (3,13)—(nowadays called in English the Kitchen Deity); the Soil *shen* or deity of place (3,21); the altar to Soil and Grain, the deity of a jurisdiction (11,25); the Altar for Rain (12,21); as well as a New Moon ritual (3,17), exorcism rituals (10,15), and prognostication rituals (13,22). This leads us to the second major term for the ancestors writ large: "Tian."

Although the term *shen* is theologically more important than Tian as the *shen* are the focus of the majority of religious rituals, Tian is mentioned more often in the *Lunyu* because of its multiple meanings, two of which are important in the text. Similarly, writings on Tian are far more common than on *shen*; a simple listing of all such studies in English alone would fill a large article. Indeed *shen* is virtually ignored in writings on Chinese Religion because the *shen* are clearly plural. In contrast, Tian can be understood as singular, although it comprehends a multitude of spiritual entities, and thus fits the Western expectation of monotheism. Moreover, by two thousand years ago, Tian had philosophical as well as theological import and thus was more attractive to Humanist Western scholars as a subject.

In the *Lunyu*, Tian is associated with the ritual offerings to the family dead (*shen*) in the home. Responding to a question regarding offerings in the home, Kongzi responds, "One who offends Tian has no place to pray" (3,13). In other words, offerings cannot be made at the family altar if one has offended the ancestors through improper behavior. The *rujia* (Confucian) worldview understood the universe to have a moral structure in and of itself; proper behavior was integral with the natural order. Tian reflected that natural order with regard to their descendants; Tian was both a natural force and a moral force. In referring to the meaning of Tian in the *Lunyu*, H. G. Creel (1949: 117) succinctly states the understanding followed in this chapter:

> All of this seems to hark back to the origin of "Heaven" [Tian] as a collective name for the great ancestors, who lived above and constantly watched the conduct of their descendants, rewarding and punishing as they pleased.

My sole caveat with this view is that the ancestors function non-anthropomorphically and the results of improper behavior are not a matter of punishment, as is often assumed by Western scholars, but of a natural response to going against the natural order. Robert Louden (2002: 79) summarizes, "*Tian* is not a personal being (much less an anthropomorphic personal being who commands us from on high)."

Regarding Tian as the conglomerate of the more important ancestral spirits and the dead central to Kongzi's sense of the progenitors of Chinese culture and exemplars of proper behavior, Kongzi said, "Tian has birthed me and provided me with *de* (virtue)" (7,23). Were it not for the mention of *de*, one could understand that Tian here stands for the compound Tiandi (Sky-Earth), which conjoined gives birth to everything. Given the mention of *de*, it is more probable that the meaning is that one is descended from and dependent upon the ancestors.

Concerning *de* as arising from proper behavior, Kongzi states that "only Tian is (truly) great" (8,19), in the context of Tian being the model for the mythic culture sage-hero/rulers. In another passage, a disciple in conversation states that "Tian set [Kongzi] on the path to sagehood" (9,6), meaning that Tian, here denoting the deceased sages in Tian, was the model for proper behavior, thus exhibiting a path that can be followed.

Kongzi complains that "No one understands me." On queried about this by a disciple, Kongzi states, "My complaint is not against Tian. . . . It is only Tian that understands me" (14,35). The meaning here is first that Kongzi does not challenge fate. The way the world turns is the way the world turns, to go against it leads to disaster and to complain about it is foolishness. But there is a second meaning here regarding Tian. As Kongzi seeks to model himself on Tian, especially its prime exemplar, the Duke of Zhou at the founding of the Zhou dynasty, he is in tune with Tian, is comprehensible to Tian. This brings us to a second major meaning of Tian in the compound *Tianming*.

Tianming is normally translated as the "Command of Heaven," with the meaning that Tian as a High God or sole God gives a particular clan the right to rule due to their virtue and removes it if the regime loses its virtue; it is often assumed to be an early Chinese doctrine of the "Divine Right of Kings." This understanding is of an anthropomorphic deity who rewards and punishes and is here disputed. In this chapter, Tian is understood as a conglomerate of ancestral spirits, and yet—and this may seem contradictory—is not an anthropomorphic deity but a deity that is closer to the cosmic order of things and thus beyond being human. In a sense, Tian is neither anthropomorphic nor non-anthropomorphic.

Literally, *ming* commonly means "command," but it can also mean "pattern." As Tian's primary meaning is "sky," the term can be understood as sky-pattern. Prognosis was a major concern of Chinese governments as far back as we can trace it. All of the brief texts we have from the Shang period are on ox scapulae and tortoise plastrons used in prognostication via pyroscapulamancy to the ancestral sprits. Similarly, the earliest Chinese book is the *Yi*, a prognostication manual to determine the way the universe is unfolding with regard to potential actions. China early made major advances in astronomy, because astrology was of considerable importance to the government for making decisions. Due to keeping astronomical records, the term for the court position of "astronomer-astrologer" became the term for "official historian."

In the *Lunyu*, an apparent aphorism is quoted: "Death and life depend on [Tian]ming; wealth and honor reside in Tian[ming]"(12,5). Here the compound is split between two parallel lines for rhetorical effect. In another passage, Kongzi says it is time for him to stop speaking. A disciple asks how his students will learn. Kongzi replies, "What does Tian say! The four seasons move [in their turn] and the myriad things arise, but what does Tian say!" (17,19). In other words, Tian being non-anthropomorphic cannot and does not speak, yet we can still learn from Tian by understanding the natural order in its moral sense. In listing his advances as the decades passed, Kongzi says, "at fifty, I understood Tianming" (2,4). Clearly, Tianming here cannot mean "Command of Heaven" but must refer to the way the cosmos is going and the proper course of action in response.

There are also passages where the meaning is ambiguous, such as 9,5 and 9,12 (the passages are too long to be provided in this brief discourse), where Tian can either be referring to its meaning as the ancestors writ large or to fate in the sense of Tianming. This suggests that at the time the *Lunyu* was being collated, the meaning of Tian was still relatively fluid, and both senses were understood as similar; hence, Tian being both anthropomorphic and non-anthropomorphic.

These meanings of Tian are found in the two major philosophical works of the *rujia* tradition a century after Kongzi. In the *Mengzi (Mencius)*, Tian is discussed in its meaning of Tianming and governance passing from one mythic sage-ruler to another. In the dialogue, we find the same expression as in the *Lunyu*, "Tian does not speak; it is through its acts and deeds that it reveals itself" (V,A,5).

In the *Xunzi*, there is a complete chapter on "Tian." Edward Machle has written a book translating and analyzing that chapter. In the following excerpt (1993: 152–53) , he focuses on Tian as Sky and thus, in a large sense, Nature itself, while still being "the preeminent *shen*":

> Tian, as the top of the cosmic hierarchy, as perfect *yang* and as the preeminent
> *shen*, is, of course, the embodiment of order, as manifested in the constant *xing*
> [form] of the heavenly bodies and seasons. Earth's order, apart from its perfect

yin and its "constant dimensions," is its response to Tian's seasons. As the ultimate source of all motion and creativity, of light and life, Tian (with Earth) is that upon which we have, in Schleiermacher's phrase, "absolute dependence." Hence it transcends all lesser beings by its essential priority—yet it has no "absolutely independent being."

Discussion

At the end of the "Introduction" above, three questions were raised. This discussion will examine each of these questions in turn.

1 Was Kongzi agnostic?

H. G. Creel noted in the early 1930s that "if a poll of Western scholars must decide on the matter, Confucius was beyond all doubt agnostic, or at least very, very skeptical" (1932: 66). Kongzi's ethics is built upon the notion of *xiao*, the crucial aspect being the ritual offerings to the ancestors. In these offerings, sincerity is of the utmost importance. If Kongzi were agnostic, the foundation of his philosophy is swept away. As Machle (1993: 25) writes concerning Xunzi:

> I find it inconceivable that Xun Qing [Xunzi] would have been so committed a Confucian, could have so revered the past, made ritual so central and treated the ancient classics as authorities, and still have rejected the religious overtones those involve; yet the interpretation widespread in recent literature would require him to do just that.

As early as 1949, Creel pointed out that interpreting passage 6,22 (see above) as "clear evidence of agnosticism . . . does not accord with the understanding of most Chinese commentators" (1949: 115).This is because if one is ethnically Chinese or comprehends Chinese culture and society, to understand Kongzi or any Chinese past or present to be agnostic concerning the theological understanding of the ancestors (*shen*) is ludicrous. To do so would mean to be agnostic about one's own existence; it is entrenched in one's sense of being.

The Chinese understanding of family, as in any tradition in which one finds Familism, includes past, present, and future. Individuals are subsumed within family and clan. As is well known, East Asians offer their names with the family at the forefront, the reverse of Western names, as it is far more important than their personal name. Their whole individual identity is based on being part of a larger social unit: family and clan. The dead of the family are integral with the living. Hence to be skeptical about the reality of the dead of the family is to question one's own existential reality.

The offering rituals are a family meal in which the deceased are the honored guests. As one is nurtured (*yang*—literally, to be breastfed) by one's parents from infancy through youth, so one cares for one's parents in old age and symbolically feeds them after death. This is the heart of *xiao*. Moreover, given that at the time of Kongzi many of the elite would have functioned in their late teens or early twenties as the Incorporator of the Dead in the clan offering ritual possessed by their late grandfather or grandmother-in-law, it is incomprehensible that they had doubts as to the reality of their *shen*. (This part of the offering ritual disappeared around twelve hundred years ago.)

The Chinese religious understanding of family is so embedded in the Chinese cultural psyche that decades of the Chinese Communist Party's attempt to destroy it failed. After the end of the Cultural Revolution, when it was realized by the Party that eliminating the Chinese understanding of family eradicated all sense of morality, the religious practices at first slowly and then rapidly returned with government approbation. The notion of a state-wide family replacing the nuclear family was not new to China. Mozi proposed it some twenty-four hundred years ago, but it was then dismissed by most Chinese intellectuals as they understood that familial love cannot be extended so broadly. Mozi's concept of *boai* (universal love) was perceived as unnatural.

Regarding Tian, in its relation to clan, the above argument also applies. In the term's meaning as Sky, here again agnosticism would be difficult to comprehend. To understand Sky and Earth as the progenitors of all that exists—as natural rather than personal forces—is found around the globe. To perceive rain from the sky entering the fertile earth and subsequently watching the plants come forth does not require faith, only rational observation. This pattern is replicated in mammals, and thus Sky is understood as male and Earth as female. Part of the problem in understanding is due to translating Tian not as "Sky" but as "Heaven." This removes Tian from being the dominant part of nature when one includes the night sky and gives it instead a Western religious meaning. The complementary opposition of Sky and Earth is replaced in Christian informed translations by Heaven and Hell. (The early Jesuit missionaries approved of the emperor's ritual offering to the male Sky but disapproved of the offering to the female Earth, since for the Jesuits, of course, God is male.) As Heaven, Tian is no longer Sky at all; it is transformed from a visible reality to a transcendental notion. But for the Chinese mind, Sky is indubitably real; one only has to look up to see it and apprehend its power over us.

Finally, there is the pragmatic argument. As mentioned in Chapter 1, if one travels around Taiwan, where Chinese Religion has continued throughout the last century uninterrupted, one will see temples dedicated to particular (non-family) deities recently refurbished and others that are derelict. The reason is simple. In the resplendent temples, people have found their pragmatic requests fulfilled and have contributed to the temple in reciprocal gratitude, whereas for those temples that are not kept up, people have not found their needs fulfilled and accordingly the temple received few donations toward its upkeep.

In the *Mengzi*, a similar attitude can be found. In a discussion on regicide not being regicide if the ruler does not act for the benefit of the governed, the example supporting the argument is that of an altar:

> When the sacrificial animals are sleek, the offerings are clean and the sacrifices are observed at due times, and yet floods and droughts come, then the altar [to the Soil and Grain *shen*] should be replaced. (VII.B.14)

Chinese language and culture promotes pragmatism and avoids non-tangibles. If Kongzi had doubts about the effectiveness of the ritual offerings to the numinous he surely would not have promoted them. This effectiveness, especially as articulated by Xunzi, primarily lies in its importance for social cohesion.

Thus, to assume that Kongzi was agnostic is to understand him from a Western rather than a Chinese cultural perspective. One can state, without qualification, that Kongzi was not agnostic concerning the actuality of *shen*, and thus his statements regarding the numinous can be taken at face value.

2 Did Kongzi have an understanding of a monotheistic deity or a "High God"?

The interrelated monotheistic traditions tend toward the understanding that Truth is absolute and singular; as God is singular, so is Truth. Accordingly, monotheism tends to be understood as a universal truth, a truth found in all cultures, at least in their initial stages before the culture descends into falsity ("paradise lost"). This is the ideological basis of ur-monotheism, first suggested by Andrew Lang and expanded by Wilhelm Schmidt over a century ago. Even when polytheism is accepted, there is still a tendency to assume a High God ruling over a hierarchical pantheon. As a literal reading of the Hebrew Bible leads to an understanding of an anthropomorphic deity, so deities elsewhere must be anthropomorphic. Since China is considered a "high civilization," it has often been assumed that they must have had a single monotheistic God or a High

God. As discussed above, many scholars in the past have considered Shangdi and Tian to be such deities in early China. This assumption continues among some scholars today, as seen, for example in the quotation from Slingerland above and by Clark and Winslett who conclude, "These few examples vindicate supernatural punishment theory's expectation, even in China, of High Deities as punishers and rewarders" (2011: 955).

High gods did develop in China in the medieval period. For example, some Daoist churches developed a hierarchical pantheon with the Jade Emperor at the pinnacle. But Daoism, along with Buddhism, over a thousand years ago became adjunct to Chinese Religion per se, comparable to the role of Freemasonry in relation to Christianity in Protestant cultures.

In earlier China, however, there is no evidence for such a concept. Robert Eno, who has studied this issue in the archaeologically excavated brief documents for decades, reiterated the findings of an earlier study (1990b) well over a decade later:

> My proposal is that the term *di* is used as a generic or collective term, assignable to any one Power or denoting groups of Powers, or all Powers, and that the Shang pantheon thus does not, in fact, possess an apex uniting its various segments. (2007: 75–6)

As for the most important theological term, *shen* as the numinous presence of the departed of family and clan, it is obvious they are multiple and cannot, by any stretch of the imagination, be conceived of as monotheistic. Even within a single family, they are still multiple: on the family altar and in the clan temples, there are from two to many individual name plaques (or two names of a couple on a single plague).

Regarding Tian, I again return to Eno for a summary statement:

> A consensus has emerged which characterizes Hsün Tzǔ's [Xunzi's] position on T'ien [Tian] by stressing that he saw T'ien not as an anthropomorphic god, but as an impersonal force of Nature, or as natural or universal law. (1990a: 131)

This, of course, is the philosophical Tian. There is also the Tian of Tiandi to whom offerings are made by the ruler and Tian as an aggregation of the departed great persons. But in no case do we have a monotheistic or high god.

3 How was the numinous both understood and engaged?

In the above discussion of the *Lunyu*, *Mengzi*, and *Xunzi*, early Chinese theology, at least of the intelligentsia, is unfolded. It is one that understands the family in and of itself to be the primary numinous entity and to which the basic religious rituals are directed. All other aspects of religion derive from this foundation. I have tried for decades, without much success, to explain this in a way that will be comprehensible to my colleagues who are not Sinologists. In the following, I will attempt to show how this early understanding remains unchanged today.

It must be pointed out that in this chapter I am explicating the theology of early *rujia* thought ("Confucianism") and the continuation of that theology into the present. China is a huge country with a very long, continuous history and over time influenced and was influenced by other cultures both on its fringes and distant, especially Buddhism. It also consisted of a number of related cultures that slowly homogenized into a general single culture and religion. Thus, there later did arise in China, especially in that Buddhism and Buddhist-influenced Daoism presented to laypersons an understanding of punitive and saving deities, of temporary hells, and of different high gods. But these are tangential to the central Chinese theology presented here and to discuss these ramifications would require a substantial book rather than a chapter.

It is difficult for those of Western culture to comprehend Chinese Religion, because different from Christianity, where major rituals take place in public churches, the most important rituals take place in the home and in clan (not public) temples, as well as at gravesites. Only close friends will be invited to be at—not participate in—the family offering and then enjoy the feast with the living members of the family. If one is only aware of public temples—local temples or temples devoted to a particular numinous entity (an anthropomorphic deity or a revered aspect of nature, such as an aged tree)—one could easily assume that aspect of Chinese Religion to be its entirety rather than peripheral to it central core.

As mentioned in the preceding, I had the good fortune to be invited to such a bimonthly offering (at the full and new moons) within a week after arriving in Taiwan as an advanced graduate student in 1965, my first experience of living in Chinese culture. I immediately realized that much of what I had read on Chinese Religion to that time, studies based on texts, was erroneous. Studies based on ethnological field work started to be published a few years later, except for the late-nineteenth-century work by de Groot which begins: "As in the case of many [peoples] . . . the human soul [*shen*] is in China the original form of all beings of a higher order. Its worship is therefore the basis of all religion in that country (1894: I,1)."

A decade later, I returned to Taiwan as a visiting professor and focused on observing clan and local temples. On subsequent trips to Taiwan and the

Chinese mainland, I explored gravesites, observed offerings there during Qingming, and, as I married into a Chinese family, took part in offerings at a gravesite in northern China, resided in Chinese homes in Taiwan and the Chinese mainland, resided in Buddhist monasteries in Taiwan thanks to a close older Chinese friend who became a Chan scholar-monk, became friends with Westerners (former Catholic monks) who became initiated Daoist priests, and observed funerals. I also began to focus on Chinese mediumism of diverse modes (Paper 1996a, 2009) and became personally familiar with a few of the many Chinese deities that arose in the last millennium—none of these were high gods or punitive.

I will conclude this section by describing the ninetieth birthday celebration of a Chinese friend of my wife that took place where I live in Victoria, B.C. She emigrated to Canada after the Vietnam War with her husband and children. They arrived penniless and began an office cleaning business that after much hard work became a success. Her children and grandchildren are all educated and successful in business or the professions, and she has great-grandchildren. She lives in a wing of her eldest son's home, with her own bedroom and a main room containing a kitchen. In a corner of her main room is a table laden with many, many photographs of her progeny set up as a virtual shrine.

For her birthday, her children brought her friends (other senior women plus myself— friendship is the fifth of the five formal filial relationships) to her home for a party, which was followed by a feast in the main part of the house with all of her children, grandchildren and great-grandchildren who lived within a reasonable distance. After the food was cooked and before it was enjoyed, it was brought into her part of the home. At her altar, she first offered the food with incense to her deceased husband, his parents and all of his ancestors (male and female). Next she offered it to the sky realm (Tian) and Guanyin. Then she offered the food to the earth realm (Di). Last she offered it to the Stove Deity.

I have never seen a person so happy; the glow that emanated from her was palpable. Having lived a very long life, she knew with complete confidence that she had been favored by the ancestors because she had acted with due propriety toward them and the family as a whole. She would die knowing that as she merged with the spirits of the family dead, she had indubitably contributed to the continuation and success of the family; she had fulfilled the religious imperative. That she has great-grandchildren ensures that offerings will continuously be made to her and the ancestors, that she will be ritually remembered far into the future.

Figure 20 Altar of woman whose ninetieth birthday was celebrated. At the top are symbols of the Sky realm, with images of Guanyin. In the middle or the human realm are pictures of (1) her deceased husband, (2) husband's parents, and (3) all the ancestors—the focus of Chinese Religion. In the lower part are placards directed to the Earth and the Stove Deity (her one-room apartment includes a kitchen).

Conclusion

The primary purpose of this chapter is to ascertain early Confucian theology through a close reading of the *Lunyu* and reference to related texts. Such a reading demonstrates that no particular theology, specifically of a monotheistic deity or a punitive High God, is embedded in the human brain or is necessary to establish a viable society. One alternative to the Western mode of theological understanding, common since the inception of horticulture in traditions uninfluenced by the religions of individual salvation, is understanding family in and of itself to be the primary numinous entity and the focus of the primary rituals. Chinese Religion is a major example of this religious modality and continues in contemporary cultures both within and without China.

Understanding a punitive deity to be necessary for the maintenance of society assumes humans to be essentially evil, a notion related to the Christian concept of Original Sin. To the contrary, *rujia* ideology assumes that humans are born oriented toward social cooperation and thus good, but corrupted by a corrupt society as found in the *Mengzi*. Alternatively, humans are innately selfish and thus bad as found in the *Xunzi*. In both texts, the solution is to educate the person back to or toward goodness. By a thousand years ago, there was a consensus that Mengzi's understanding is the correct one and that has since been the primary understanding in China.

Until several decades ago, one could not be a witness at a trial in the United States or Canada if one was an atheist, as it was assumed that no one would tell the truth if there was no fear of divine punishment—that is, the assumption was that humans are inherently sinful. In literary Chinese, the logograph for truth is a combination of the pictograph for a person and the sign for speech. In other words, it is assumed that speaking the truth is part of the natural moral order, and people will normally speak truthfully as they are inherently good. Hence, there is neither a need for nor a concept of a punitive High God to compel a person to speak the truth or, for that matter, do good.

5

The Role of Possession Trance in Chinese Culture and Religion: A Comparative Overview from the Neolithic to the Present

Introduction

Contemporary scholars of Chinese Religion who carry out fieldwork find mediumism (spirit possession) a common aspect of the Chinese religious gestalt. This is in contrast to an earlier generation of scholars whose study, for most, was based on texts and who had little or no experience of Chinese Religion as a living tradition. Interpretations and understandings of Chinese Religion by those experiencing Chinese Religion, on the whole, are compatible with Chinese scholars living in Chinese contexts, while the understandings arising from Western or Western-influenced text-based scholarship tend to be at odds with the Chinese understanding, as well as Chinese commentaries on the same texts. Perhaps on no topic has this discrepancy been greater than with that of mediumism.

The earlier studies tended to understand mediumism, when it was recognized at all, as a peripheral phenomenon affecting few, all lacking in education, who were socially marginal and/or mentally ill. This perception was read into the thinking of the traditional elite, who were understood to be agnostic toward the spirit realm, if not atheistic, reflecting the viewpoint of the Western scholars with regard to their own, often liberal Protestant with Humanist leanings, religio-cultural background.

In contrast, a century ago, J. J. M. de Groot (1894,vol. 6: 1187–341), the first Western scholar to ground his study of Chinese Religion on observation, found mediumism so ubiquitous that he termed normative Chinese Religion, "Wuism," referring to a common term for mediums in the classical literature: *wu*. Searching through the Chinese literature, de Groot found numerous references to mediumism, these being the first clearly described religious experiences in early Chinese texts. I do not agree with all of de Groot's interpretations in these regards and certainly not with his attitude. Still, he is the first scholar to apply the beginning of participant-observation methodologies to the study of Chinese Religion and understood Chinese Religion far more perceptively than other Western scholars of his day.

Somehow, de Groot's voluminous and thorough studies had little effect on Sinology as a whole. Some well-known Sinologists, normally excellent scholars, being unfamiliar with the phenomenon and language of spirit possession, completely misread references to mediumism, thus not passing on examples of spirit possession among the educated. Moreover, even popular armchair theoreticians of shamanism, the most commonly cited being Eliade, who does distinguish between mediums and shamans in theory, confuse the two with regard to early China (for a critique and contrary understanding of Eliade, see Paper 1995b: 51–83). This misunderstanding led to the imputation of shamanism in early China, with no clear evidence for such religious behavior, leading to a number of interesting but superficial assumptions about Shang religion and government in that regard, as well as about Chu culture. Lack of a comparative background among earlier scholars of Chinese culture did not allow an understanding that Chinese mediumism fits into a religio-political complex that is widespread, including most, if not all, agricultural civilizations.

The Chinese pattern is not only duplicated in the sub-Saharan African kingdoms (a complex of spirit possession, ritual use of alcohol, the feeding of ancestors, and clan-based kingship), but spirit possession was certainly present in the supposed roots of Western civilization: there are indisputable references to the phenomenon in biblical accounts of Israelite religio-politics (see 1 Samuel 28); the description of behavior in Euripides' *Bacchae* can only be referring to possession trance; and it was part and parcel of Hellenic and normative Roman religion. Almost certainly, for example, the Delphic oracle was possessed by Apollo. Mediumism is an important part of indigenous religion throughout East Asia, South Asia, West Asia, Oceania, and Africa. Accordingly, although spirit possession cannot be explicitly documented earlier than 2,500 years ago in China, an understanding of the probable origins of mediumism and its relation to Chinese culture can allow us to posit a much earlier date.

It is the fortuitous collaboration of a then text-based historian of religion, Daniel Overmyer, with an anthropologist studying Chinese Religion, David Jordan, along with the work of revisionist scholars that led to an awakening within Chinese studies in the West to the importance of mediumism. Since the publication of that collaboration, Overmyer (2002: 315) has presented mediumism as part and parcel of normative, syncretic, Chinese Religion: "In the village context Guanyin was worshipped for family protection, the *Diamond sūtra* was recited to bring good harvests, and Confucian-style 'masters of ceremonies' cooperated with spirit-mediums to help make rituals effective."

A theoretical discourse on the inception of mediumism

Given that ecstatic religious functionaries, that is, those whose religious functioning involves trance, are virtually ubiquitous in human cultures—even in Protestant Christian tradition which more than any other religious tradition in general eschews ecstasy, there are a number of modes, such as Pentecostalism, which focus on direct ecstatic experience of the divine—one can posit a theoretical history of its development from a comparative standpoint. In this section, an outline of this hypothetical development will be presented with a focus on mediumism. (For a far more complete discourse on the functional religious ecstasy in general, see Paper 2004: 31–51.)

From the ethnographic literature, it seems that most, if not all, gathering-hunting traditions ritually avoid the dead. For example, some gathering-hunting traditions around the northern Great Lakes, after a year's mourning, held a final feast for the deceased and then asked the spirit of the deceased not to return. Yet, within the same tradition, there may still be an understanding that the dead of the family can mediate with the spirit realm. At a Winnebago funeral, within the speech enumerating the final offerings to the dead, we find, "Now here are these things, and in return we ask you to act as mediator (between the spirits and us) [as the soul journeys to the realm of the dead, far away from the living]" (Radin 1923: 92–107).

Horticulture-hunting traditions, to the contrary, revere the dead. As examples, some traditions grind up the bones of the family dead and mix them into a drink to be ingested by the living family members; others bury the bones in large communal pits. Prior to the arrival of Europeans, Iroquoian speaking cultures around the eastern Great Lakes, when it was time to move due to depleted fields every ten to fifteen years, brought all the corpses buried in the related villages together and buried them, following elaborate ceremonies, in a large ossuary (see Trigger 1976: 85–90).

The reason for this difference is not difficult to understand. For gathering-hunting traditions living a semi-nomadic existence in small groups, the corpse is a spiritually potent element irrelevant to their subsistence patterns, which are dependent on animal and plant spirits (who may at times appear in anthropomorphic form). Horticultural-hunting cultures tend to reside in large matrilineal/matrilocal clan dwellings near the clan gardens. The dead contribute to the strength of the clan and are buried close to the living to enhance clan continuity.

Gathering-hunting traditions usually interrelate with the spirit realm through shamanism. While shamanic trances can involve the incorporation of helping animal spirits, such incorporation does not displace the human spirit within the body. Those in shamanic trance may dance the movements of the animal spirits but simultaneously remain themselves. As horticulture becomes more important than hunting, theriomorphic spirits give way to anthropomorphic ones. In early agricultural societies, the transition becomes complete, and ancestral spirits take on effective roles. Incorporation of anthropomorphic spirits is different from that of theriomorphic spirits as the human spirits fit comfortably into human bodies. Moreover, there would be far more equanimity with the incorporation of a dead family member, a beloved grandmother or grandfather, than of a potentially dangerous nonhuman spirit. Such incorporation could become temporarily total, allowing the dead family elder to continue to directly advise the family. Given centuries, if not millennia of familiarity with spirit possession by the family dead, as other spirits become anthropomorphized, so too they can directly interrelate with the human community through trance possession.

At the earliest known urban agricultural site to date, Çatalhöyük in central Anatolia, dating to ca. 9000 BP, dead adults were buried under the sleeping platforms of the homes, while children were buried under the floors (Staff: 26). The simplest explanation is that this practice would enhance the opportunity for people to communicate with the dead in their dreams and, perhaps, to be possessed by them. Children were not needed for advice and were buried to keep them nearby but not within the beds. It is quite possible that mediumism was present in Çatalhöyük; certainly it was later omnipresent throughout the area.

In the earliest agricultural civilization for which we have written records regarding ritual roles, Sumeria, the "Lady Deity" (*nin-dinger*) was probably the female high priest. She was of elevated social status and would probably have been possessed by the deity Inanna (in later periods, Ishtar), who had ritual intercourse with her divine consort Dumuzi (later Tammuz), represented by or incarnated in the king. By the historical period, the "Sacred Marriage Rite" functioned as the validation of Mesopotamian kingship. In cities aside from Inanna's Uruk, the woman participating in the ritual was usually possessed by the female protector deity of the city or the consort of the city's male protector deity. Most commonly, she was identified with Inanna/Ishtar in order to associate the city's ruler with the powerful female deity (see Paper 1997: chap. 3).

Mediumism and agriculture went hand in hand throughout the world, save possibly for the Americas. In the latter area, all the other attributes regarding the dead are found, except that shamanism seems not to have been displaced by mediumism. However, our knowledge of the nature of ritual trance of the agricultural civilizations is quite limited due to the Spanish destruction of the Native libraries. Nonetheless, the continuing indigenous religions of the non-elite are definitely shamanic.

The Inception of mediumism in China

The understanding of early China is now far more complex than it was a half-century ago. China covers a large area and was the home of at least two major incipient civilizations, as well as a number of other cultures and subcultures. By two thousand years ago, much of the area shared many features of a homogeneous religion and culture, resulting from centuries of synthesis, due to the common desire of all empires to promote stability via a standard religio-culture. Hence, Constantine promoted Christianity, Ashoka promoted Buddhism, and the Inca promoted a synthesized Andean tradition. Similarly, the Han emperors sought to culturally stabilize their expanding empire. The disparate roots of this continuing tradition in China still remain far from clear.

In Japan and Korea, mediumism is closely tied to wet-rice agriculture. While the latter evidences Altaic shamanistic practices in the earliest kingdoms, a myth seems to relate the inception of mediumism to the spread of wet-rice cultivation (Chang 1977: 136–50). Hence, although there has been but limited study to date of the origination of wet-rice agriculture in the Yangtze River basin, it seems reasonable to assume, although there is no specific evidence as yet, that mediumism would have also been present quite early.

In the past, there was much discussion regarding shamanistic imagery in texts attributed to that region, particularly the early strata of the *Zhuangzi* and the *Lisao* (Encountering Sorrow). However, these specific terms, focusing on trance-flight, are not found in any context of functional shamanism, but rather exist as metaphors to either make philosophical points or for poetic imagery. Accordingly, these terms cannot be used to indicate the practice of shamanism at the time they were written. They may be vestiges through cultural memory of either much earlier practices or of concepts that filtered south from Siberia. Yet a small number of shamans continue to function in southern China, within the context of mediumism, and some mediums also function shamanistically as well. As I have discussed in previous studies (Paper 1995b: 52–60, 132–40), this is more likely due to individual temperament rather than religio-cultural differences.

In the millet-based agricultural civilization of the north, until the Zhou period, again there are hints from iconography of shamanistic imagery, but much that has been read into Shang and earlier culture, including my own early work on the topic, is extremely speculative. Again, analyses of single logographs involve more imagination than certainty.

In late Zhou texts there are a number of references to spirit possession, and these have been collected by de Groot, as mentioned above. By at least the mid-Zhou period, court officials included mediums, and these governmental offices continued into the Tang period. By that time, these were normally the only official roles that females maintained (as in some African kingdoms), save for the complementary ritual roles of wives of rulers, etc. Many of these references were misunderstood by Western scholars, being unfamiliar with mediumism. To give but a single example, much has been made of exposing female religious functionaries out in the burning sun during prolonged drought. (The earliest reference is *Zuozhuan*, "Xigong," year 21; given the context, it is unclear if this was an actual practice or a rhetorical metaphor.) This would be inexplicable unless it was a possessed medium that was exposed, so that the deity responsible for the lack of rain could directly experience the suffering, not the medium herself, and this, indeed, is the Chinese understanding, as expressed in Han texts (in De Groot: vol. 6: 1193–94).

In an earlier study, I have argued that the ritual texts, put together in the early Han period, require an understanding that the ritual role of the *shi* (Incorporator of the Dead, usually but strangely translated as "Impersonator of the Dead") involved spirit possession of the *shi* by the major recipient of a clan sacrifice, and that such behavior is implied by the sacrificial odes in the *Shi*, gathered in the early Zhou period. This would mean that many, perhaps the majority, of the elite (both male and female), usually in their late teens to early twenties, would have experienced possession by the clan ancestors, strengthening their bonding with the clan (see Paper 1995b: 85–124). Hence, while it is likely that shamanism was present very early on in northern China contiguous to northeastern Asia, all explicit references to functional ecstatic religious experience in the earliest texts make far more sense as referring to mediumism, but this takes us back roughly three thousand years only. We cannot state how early mediumism might have occurred, but obviously for mediumism to become an important aspect of Chinese Religion required centuries if not longer. Parallels with other traditions certainly suggest the presence of mediumism in central and southern China much earlier, dating to the development of horticulture.

The last two thousand years: Functional mediumism

Regardless of the antiquity of mediumism in China, by the time we have descriptive texts, mediumism was sufficiently important in the culture that there were several terms for such offices in the government, indicating either regional variation, or more likely, different modes of specialization. Mediums not only functioned through spirit possession but also served as subsidiary priests in the offering rituals, as exorcists, and in other religious roles.

The earliest precise statement that spirit possession is the key factor in these offices is found in the *Guoyu* (Discourses of the States: Qiyuxia):

> . . . those among the people whose souls were not flighty and were able to be reverential and inwardly upright, their wisdom could interpret the upper (Sky) and lower (Earth) realms; their sanctity was able to enlighten the distant, proclaiming it with clarity; their intelligence was able to illuminate it (divine and/or bring forth benevolent spirits); their cleverness was able to understand and eliminate it (exorcise maleficent spirits). For this reason, the bright spirits (deceased clan luminaries) descended into (possessed) them; if [they descended] into a male, [he] was called *xi*; if into a female, [she] was called *wu*. [The Han ritual texts instead refer to "male *wu*" and "female *wu*."] (Unless otherwise noted by reference to another scholar, all translations from the Chinese texts are my own.)

Both from the ritual odes and when the spirits involved in possession are named, there is no indication that these "bright spirits" (*mingshen*) and "spirits" (*shen*) are those of any other than important clan dead until later in Chinese history.

A more explicit description of spirit possession, as valid today as in the past, is found in the debunking works of Wang Chong (27–97 CE), who does not deny possession in and of itself (*Lunheng* [Discourses Weighed in the Balance]: ch. 20):

> The dead of past generations place people in trance and use them to speak. When the *wu* pray with mysterious sounds they bring down the souls of the dead, who speak through the mouths of the *wu*. All their words are but boastfulness.

As the central government gained unified control and the *ru* gained a monopoly on government offices, mediumism disappears from government and the state-sanctioned sacrifices. The sacrificial role of the Incorporator of the Dead is gone by the early Tang, and state offices for mediums no longer exist in the Song period (Davis 2001: 188).

On the other hand, the incorporation of large parts of East Asia into China, particularly the southern part, during the Han dynasty appears to have caused an increase in the importance of mediumistic behavior. The *Shiji* (ch. 12), in referring to the conquering of Yue, not only mentions frequent rituals involving possession by ghosts (*gui*), but places these rituals in the context of divination with cocks, a common combination of religious practices throughout sub-Saharan Africa and southern Asia.

While we have descriptions of the government offices, mediumism outside of the government in the early period is less clear. Certainly the roles of mediums remained central to Chinese Religion despite a lack of government support and later antagonism. The *wu* not only functioned as mediums but had priestly roles in the carrying out of both government and community (nonofficial) rituals. The latter is evident from negative descriptions by later writings of the *ru*, many of whom seemed to have disparaged nonofficial rites. *Wu* also functioned as healers, as they do today. Indeed, the importance of mediums may have increased with changes in Chinese Religion regarding the nature of deities.

The anthropomorphization of nature deities begins early in China. The earliest reference seems to be in the *Zuozhuan* (Chronicles of Mr. Zuo) (Zhao, twenty-ninth year, 4). In this passage, the altars to Land and Grain are linked to specific humans with biographies. The sacrifices were made to the deceased humans-become-nature-deities; however, these deities were not linked with spirit possession. From all the available evidence, possessing spirits prior to the Song period seem to be limited to dead humans (here further research would create more certainty). For example, possessing spirits (*shen*) are not always named, but in the *Hanshu*, we find mention of a female *wu* being possessed by a spirit (*shen*) in 86 BCE, who was a specific former emperor. This fits my theory discussed above that full possession can only be by anthropomorphic spirits. In or by the Song, most of the deities come to be understood as similar to ancestral spirits, that is, dead human beings with biographies (see Hansen 1990 for examples). Although theriomorphic spirits continued in importance, since the Song, they were conceived of as anthropomorphized. For example, all of the images of fox deities I observed (in 1993) in Sinicized Manchurian homes were in human form.

The almost complete anthropomorphization of deities (certain cosmic deities are not anthropomorphized, but they do not possess humans) may be due to the integration of Sinicized Buddhism into the Chinese religious gestalt. That is, the understanding of Buddhist effective spirits, who are predominantly Boddhisattvas (enlightened humans), may have stimulated the understanding that efficacious deities are also dead human beings. This shift in understanding not only allows mediums to be possessed by the souls of ancestors but by the deities as well. Prior to this transformation, while mediums presided over communal sacrifices to nature and other spirits, there is but partial suggestion in the literature that they were possessed by them. For example, an exception would be deities responsible for rain, who may already have been anthropomorphized.

The negative attitude of the *ru* was not only due to political competition, as well as the elite looking down on the *wu* officials, who probably were not from elite backgrounds, but also due to the increasingly negative orientation toward females, particularly in public roles. Wang Fu (second century CE), in his *Qianfu lun* (Discourses of a Recluse) (chap. 3), complaining of women at ease in public instead of being busy in the home, noted that many *wu* were either married or unmarried women who began their practice in the home but then took on public functions. By the end of the Ming dynasty, well over a millennium later, women were not only forbidden public roles (see Huang 1084: 609), but mediums were forbidden to practice, although the ethnohistorical record makes clear that these prohibitions were not effectively enforced (see deGroot).

While rituals, including mediumistic ones, outside of those approved by the state were increasingly proscribed, in large part due to fear of sedition, mediumism did continue within the Daoist churches. Indeed, the development of *Daojiao* may, in part, be due to the *fangshi* as well as the *wu*, who were forced out of office by the eunuchs during the political turmoil leading to the end of the Han, forming their own religio-political movements. When these movements were militarily defeated by the generalissimo Cao Cao, whose son created the Wei dynasty, the religious aspects seem to have continued within the formation of the Daoist churches. The Daoist churches from their inception included spirit possession among the initiated. The practice continues in the present, as I have been privately informed by an initiated female *daoshi* (Daoist priest).

Edward L. Davis (2001) has persuasively argued that while the role of court mediums disappeared at the end of the Tang, many of their activities were taken over by Buddhist and Daoist clergy in a synthesis with local mediums throughout the Song. Davis's book is the most important historical study of mediumism in China since de Groot a century earlier. Davis's study also details the development of the role of the *fangshi* within mediumism, a role which continues in contemporary practices, although it seems to be earlier than he suggests (see above). His work resolves many of the issues in understanding the important changes that took place in these regards during the Song, which led to Chinese Religion as we know it today.

The last two thousand years: Corollary aspects

Although at least some *ru* disparaged mediums among the common people, this did not necessarily mean that the *ru* in general were antagonistic toward spirit possession in and of itself. If my theory that the Incorporator of the Dead was possessed by the ancestral recipient of the sacrifice is correct, then the elite in general were intimately familiar with possession well into the medieval period. Moreover, after many of the elite migrated to the southern half of China following the loss of the north to non-Chinese forces, many of the landed gentry were closely connected with the emerging Daoist churches in which various forms of possession trance, including spirit-writing (writing in trance via spirit possession), were practiced. Writing was the essence of elite self-identification. As elite status increasingly was based on *rujia*-oriented education, to be an elite meant to be a *wenren*, a literatus. The literati have continuously been connected with spirit-writing, being fascinated by spirit-writing from its beginning in the early Daoist churches and writing in trance themselves in the spirit-writing cults which continue to today.

While undoubtedly but a minority of the literati involved themselves in possession-trance writing, virtually all of the elite have been highly influenced by the aesthetic consequence of spirit-writing. The calligraphy of early Daoist spirit-writing, combined with earlier Chinese poetry using shamanistic imagery to connote freedom, along with metaphors deriving from the ecstatic experience of nothingness, became not only the basis of elite aesthetics, but the means of expressing all that is pertinent to *Daojia* thought as the complement of *rujia* thought (see Paper 1995b: 157–95).

The basis of Chinese visual arts aesthetics is traditionally traced back to a father and son of one of the two most powerful families in southern China of the fourth century. The Taizong emperor of the Tang dynasty (r. 626–49) and his appointed adviser Chu Suiliang (597–658) are responsible for basing the aesthetic standards on purported examples of these individuals' calligraphy.

Both Wang Xizhi (321–78) and his youngest son, Wang Xianzhi (344–88), were followers of the "Way of the Celestial Master" (*Tianshidao*), a major Daoist sect. The two medieval critics responsible for propagating the tradition of the Wangs, Yang Xin (370–442) and Tao Hongjing (456–536), were also important in the development of institutional Daoism. Daoism reinforced the very early tradition of writing for communication with spirits and introduced aspects of calligraphic style as essential features of their sacred manuscripts and spiritual petitions (Chen 1932: 439–66).

Mao Shan Daoism developed at this time, and its founder, Yang Xi (b. 330), practiced spirit-writing, which led to the formalization of *caoshu* (a free, rapid, fluid style earlier used for quick writing of notes, etc.) as a calligraphic style, which the Wangs preferred. Stylistic connections have been noted between Wang Xianzhi and Yang Xi, and the former's calligraphy was later noted for its spontaneity. Xie Lingyun (385–433), the originator of landscape poetry, was a noted calligrapher as well and also closely associated with the "Way of the Celestial Master." Hence, the origin of the classic tradition of calligraphy arises from fourth-century developments relating to the literary mode of spirit possession (see Ledderose 1977, 1979).

It was during the Song period that the Chinese aesthetic styles and standards were set for all time. The person most influential in this development was Mi Fu (1052–1107). Through his critical works and in his own calligraphy, Mi Fu reinforced the tradition of basing the aesthetic standard for brushwork on the two Wangs. Mi Fu and his colleague, Su Shi (1037–1101), together with several friends, applied this aesthetic of calligraphy to the closely related activity of painting as a literati avocation. As an eminent Chinese art historian has stated, "The more painting emphasized inner experience and resembled calligraphy, the more it devalued representational context in favor of the purely aesthetic" (Fong 1976: 91).

Su Shi was one of the major Chinese poets of all time; he was an important official (when not in political exile), leader of the conservative faction in Song politics, considered one of the Song dynasty's Four Masters of calligraphy, an amateur painter, and was involved with Daoism. His paintings were apparently created spontaneously after attaining an alcoholic trance. (This should not be understood as a possession trance.) Mi Fu wrote of him:

> When I first saw him, he was slightly drunk and said: "Could you paste this paper on the wall? It is Kuan-yin paper." Then he rose and made two bamboos, a bare tree, and a strange rock. (Bush 1971: 9)

Another painter described Su Shi's tendency at literary gatherings to fall asleep after several cups of wine, then arise and rapidly paint (Lin 1947: 277).

Major Yuan dynasty painters also left poems reflecting the Northern Song literati aesthetic based on non-possession-trance experiences. Wu Zhen (1280–1354) wrote, "When I begin to paint I am not conscious of myself / And am completely unaware of the brush in my hand" (Bush 1971: 132). These approaches to brushwork were continually reinforced by the later Ming and Qing theorists.

Hence, the literati were involved not only directly with spirit possession through the role of the Incorporator of the Dead into the medieval period, as well as with spirit-writing through trance possession from the beginning of institutional Daoism to the present, but increasingly with an aesthetic mode of calligraphy and painting that derived from spirit-writing and other trance experiences. Of course, these other trance experiences, such as those of Su Shi, are not to be understood as involving spirit possession. This mode of aesthetics was integral to the literati ideology that existed in complementary opposition to the ideology pertinent to holding government office. The nonconscious and therefore spontaneous mode of calligraphy in which all the elite, the scholar-officials, were adept to some degree, served as a complementary but opposite activity to those of the official realm—the spontaneity (*ziran*) of Daoist thought and, since the Tang, Chan Buddhism, as opposed to the ritual order (*li*) of official life.

Sex/Gender aspects

Possibly the earliest explicit reference to spirit possession anywhere is in the Hebrew Bible (1 Samuel 28). Saul, urgently needing the advice of Samuel, his recently deceased adviser, specifically calls for a female medium, so that he can speak directly with Samuel. The previously mentioned bacchantes as well as the Delphic oracle were all female (or males dressed as females). Throughout Africa, as well as South and East Asia, mediums have been predominantly female. In Korea, those few males who take on the roles of a *mudang* or *mansin* wear female garb while performing. In African-Brazilian Candomblé many of the small number of males, in comparison to women who are possessed (a large number of males are involved in other roles), are understood to be passive homosexuals. That most spirit mediums are female is not a matter of cultural predilection, it is a human constant, save where females are forbidden from such public roles, and males step into the religious vacuum.

As I have argued elsewhere, based on the nearly identical statements of reflective mediums in widely disparate cultures, this cultural constant is due to general neurophysiological differences between males and females, and at least one of the genes involved may have been identified. While such a statement may be politically incorrect in the present academic climate, it is the only explanation that fits the data perfectly. Females more easily go into trance than males, even in shamanistic cultures. Males usually require ritual activity and/or ritual props to place themselves in trance; experienced female mediums and shamans can do so instantly. This is a phenomenon I have personally observed cross-culturally. But articulate female mediums add to this phenomenon the importance of a female nurturing personality in being receptive to possession by spirits, even if they are childless themselves.

In misogynist Western culture, these attributes have been interpreted as negative; hence, Western feminists in general eschew discussing biological differences between the sexes. In a classic work in social anthropology, I.M. Lewis (1971) has argued that females take on these roles in northern Africa because these are the only means of prestige available to them. I think the Chinese data, when not interpreted from the standpoint of Western ethnocentrism, as well as the data from Africa and elsewhere, indicates that mediumistic roles are far from being limited to the socially marginal and in many of these cultures women are also highly valued. If my theory of the origin of mediumism is correct, then the practice arose in matrifocal cultures, as egalitarian horticultural societies are generally matrilineal and matrilocal, in contradistinction to gender hierarchy in class-structured agricultural situations. Women functioned as mediums, not only because of inherently superior abilities to do so, but because it was women who were most closely linked to the then, and continuing in some African kingdoms and Native American traditions, matrilineal and matrilocal clans.

Returning to China, we find that the lowering of the status of females was a gradual development. From the Shang through the very early Han, tombs of female elite can be as elaborate as those of males. There is nothing to suggest in the classical ritual texts that the *wu* officials were looked down upon because they were predominantly female. And in same texts, the consort of the ruler was as important to the sacrificial rites as the ruler. During the Han, women held other offices temporarily, including that of the *shi* (Astrologer-Historian). But by the end of the Han, there is clear evidence that females were devalued in relation to males. China is an example of patrilineal warrior clans in the context of kingship developing patriarchy. But it was not until the reformation of *rujia* during the Song that the restrictions on females outside of the home became severe. Chinese patriarchy required several thousand years of development to attain its height, and it never reached the degree of misogyny evident in Christian culture.

The point of this discussion is that the seeming growth of negativity toward mediumism from the end of the Han may be due more to the sex of the mediums, as well as the gender orientation of the profession, than to the activity itself. To be a medium outside of the home is to function publicly, and a *rujia* principle, to protect the stability of the family, was that females were to remain inside the family compound. If non-elite women were to be in public for various sorts of employment, they were not to congregate in public spaces such as temples and certainly were not to direct or be the focus of rituals. Were it not for the fact that women were at the center of mediumism, perhaps the general attitude of the Chinese elite toward non-elite mediumism, particularly from the Song period on, would have been more benign.

The importance of Chinese mediumism: Today and the future

I will never forget, when I first began to do fieldwork on mediums in Taiwan decades ago, speaking to temple officials in the office of a Mazu "mother"-temple in the mountains of central Taiwan about mediumistic activities at the temple. Just as the head of the temple was assuring me that such activities never take place at the temple, the first of a series of visits by Mazu's from "daughter"-temples arrived, replete with their possessed mediums within the noisy processions. The temple officials and I just looked at each other, none of us speaking a word. I have rarely been at a large, busy temple in Taiwan, at least since the end of martial law, without observing both expected and unplanned spirit possessions. Yet this common mode of religious behavior was assiduously kept from foreign observers when possible. Knowing the modern Western abhorrence of ecstatic religious behavior, this was considered one of China's ignoble secrets. One is reminded of the illegality of eating dog (a ritual food) in Taiwan prior to the end of martial law due to Western rather than Chinese values.

Shortly after the end of martial law in Taiwan over two decades ago, thousands of women came out of the closet, so to speak, and began to function as mediums; thousands more began to take up the practice. Thus, a predominantly female religious role is again flourishing after a millennium of suppression. Female mediums find themselves free from many social constraints and the availability of these renewed behaviors accords well with modern Chinese feminism.

"Western modernization" has not had the expected (by Westerners) impact in these regards. In spite of the ready availability of both modern Western and sophisticated Chinese medicine, large numbers of people also seek succor from the relevant deities through possessed mediums. Given Chinese culture's deserved reputation for pragmatism, obviously, many Chinese find these methods effective. Furthermore, modern education and global business practices have not led to the demise of mediumistic behavior among the elite; I have found contemporary healing practitioners utilizing spirit-writing to include university deans and bank vice-presidents. Similarly, on the Mainland, spirit possession has been visible since at least the late 1980s (see Dean 1993: 64ff).

Unable to suppress the resurgence of mediumism, the government in Taiwan decided to co-opt it. Shortly after the end of martial law the government urged the creation of a government-recognized society of mediums who call themselves *lingji*, with a registration of members (there are several thousand), a charter, officers, etc. (see Paper 1996a: 105–29). Concerned about the low esteem of ordinary mediums, this new society has worked to raise their social status. It has created a college to educate mediums, and its first president earned a PhD (dissertation published, see Lai 1999). Hence, many mediums, although far from all, are now working within modern forms of social organization. The traditional *jitong* mediums of Taiwan, members of most spirit-writing temples, as well as other mediums, however, are not part of this organization.

Given all of these developments, there is no reason to assume that mediumism will weaken anytime in the foreseeable future. Government attempts at suppression have never been successful, class distinctions but influence the type of spirit possession, and modern developments, particularly with regard to transportation and communications, but enhance the opportunities for expansion.

Conclusion

Barring de Groot's pioneering studies, until relatively recently, studies of Chinese Religion, when they have dealt with mediumism at all, have treated it as peripheral and the result of ignorance, low-class status, and/or mental instability. More recent studies have realized that the educated elite were also participants and that the practice is important in the Chinese religious gestalt. The historical perspective of this chapter is intended to demonstrate that mediumism has long been and remains an essential feature of Chinese Religion.

De Groot understood "wuism" to be part of an overall Asian "animism," a term that, fortunately, has almost disappeared into the dustbin of ethnocentric scholarship. But he was partially correct; Chinese mediumism is part of a larger, more global, construct. This is a general religious complex centered on clan ancestors with rituals focusing on feeding the family dead, alcoholic beverages to enhance the trance states of the living, and offerings to the dead, in addition to spirit possession by ancestors or deities who were once humans. Included in this religious complex, where there are caste-stratified societies, is the notion that the legitimate ruler is the clan head, whose ritual role as the chief priest of the politically superior clan expands into the political role of king. In other words, the construct aptly termed "gods, ghosts and ancestors" (Jordan 1972: book title) is found in all agricultural societies worldwide that are essentially unchanged by the spread of the proselytizing, universal religions: Buddhism, Christianity, and Islam. (The indigenous civilizations of the Americas may be a slight exception, solely with regard to the aspect of mediumism, but given that Native empires were destroyed a half-millennium ago by Christian Spain, it is unclear as to how far shamanism may have shaded into mediumism. In the Andes, the mummified dead rulers, males and females, were fed daily, and their advice was sought by their living kin, and the Pueblo *katchina* are essentially ancestors or ghosts.) Diffusion is not suggested; rather, it is proposed that this is a consequence of particular developments within a religio-ecological framework.

All of these traditions are highly pragmatic with regard to religion. The family dead are not theoretical constructs; they are those of memory or were the memories of those of our memory. The common notion of family extends into time as well as space. The concept of family includes the valuing of those with extensive experience, those who have survived long enough to be elders. Our need for their advice continues after their death, and given the predilection of humans for trance experiences, we developed trances that allowed for our family dead to temporarily inhabit our bodies so that we could (and can) converse with them and receive their advice. Nature and other spirits over time become transformed into dead humans so that they too can possess us. As David Jordan and others have long since indicated, ghosts become gods through demonstrating their goodwill via benevolent possession.

Given a multiplicity of spirits, we can pick and choose among them for those who are willing and/or able to best help us. The perceived effectiveness of a deity can easily be determined by examining the state of their temples in China when their care is in the hands of the people. If a temple is in good repair and flourishing, then one can be certain that the deity has benefited many. If the temple is in a state of decay, the deity has not recently been of benefit to people and has not received gifts in return. As Mengzi (VII.B.14) stated long ago, in the context of justifying regicide,

> If the sacrificial animals are perfect, the bowls of millet are pure, and the sacrifices are offered in their proper season, and yet there are floods or droughts, then the deities of land and grain should be dismissed and replaced by others.

Similarly, if mediumism were not the most effective means to communicate and receive benefits from the deities then that method would also have long since been replaced.

The advantage of mediumism is that it makes religion tangible; it allows us to actually speak with and be touched by the dead of the family and deities. It is the height of Western ethnocentrism to assume that the ancestral spirits and deities of the Chinese are not real, that they cannot actually appear in the bodies of mediums to assist and bless living humans. Making judgments about the validity of religious understanding and experience is not a proper topic for religious studies. Obviously, for the pragmatic Chinese, the deities are effective, as they are for Western observers open to the Chinese experiences.

In summary, mediumism cannot be separated out of the Chinese religious gestalt. It is not optional or peripheral. It has been central to the tradition from its beginning thousands of years ago and will continue to be so as long as Chinese Religion remains viable. Moreover, the religious complex in which mediumism is found determines that Chinese Religion, in general, is far from unique and shares many interconnected features within a religious pattern once found in virtually all civilizations and continuing in traditional Polynesian and sub-Saharan African religions.

6

State and Religion in China: The District Magistrate as Priest

Introduction

An essential aspect of Chinese civilization, at least since the formation of Chinese kingdoms over 3,500 years ago, is state religion, which became highly formalized by the beginning of the Chinese empire over 2,200 years ago. As used in this book, "state religion" does not mean a religion designated to be the official religion of the state as found, for example, in the Christian tradition in which state and religion are understood to be separate yet can be partnered, such as the Church of England. Rather, here state religion refers to those countries in which religion is an integral part of culture, including governance, as found in pre-Western-dominated East Asia, sub-Saharan Africa, the Americas, Polynesia, and other areas, and earlier throughout the Mediterranean world. Much as *huaren jiao* (Chinese Religion) has in the main been misrepresented in the West for half a millennium due to Jesuit missionaries creating a triune "Three Chinese Religions," the state religion, until recently (see, Nylan and Wilson 2010), has been virtually ignored. Indeed, the traditional Chinese state tends to be understood as nonreligious and the contemporary state is officially atheistic (but atheism should not be confused with non-religion, Familism itself not being theistic). This chapter seeks to counter this understanding by focusing on the local aspect of Chinese state religion. (For an in-depth study of the imperial aspect, see the work of Chen Shuguo 2010.)

I have previously written on the role of the Chinese emperor as the chief priest of the empire (Paper 1995b: Chapter 2). Both family and state religion modeled itself on the very early offering rituals to clan ancestors. The state became perceived as the family writ large, so that the clan offerings of the emperor were, in effect, state rituals, and the emperor made offerings on behalf of the people to cosmic and nature spirits. But the government went even further by controlling other institutionalized religions adjunct to Chinese Religion and by co-opting popular religion by granting titles to popular deities. For example, Mazu, the popular sea and mercantile deity of the southeast coastal area, was granted several titles by the government over the last thousand years, including Queen of Sky, making her an official deity. More recently, the contemporary government continued this practice in the modern global context by successfully applying to UNESCO in 2009 for Mazu to be granted the status of an Intangible Cultural Heritage. This was hardly the action of a secular, let alone atheistic, government. She is the only deity itself to date, I understand, officially recognized by an agency of the United Nations.

Local state religion

The beginning of John R. Watts' oft-cited *The District Magistrate in Late Imperial China* (1972: 11–12) states, "The function of the district magistrate was to take charge of all matters affecting the maintenance of public order." Although the book notes that Chinese sources list "sacrifice to spirits" among the magistrate's functions, Watts only discusses "judicial and fiscal affairs." In the Chinese understanding, the magistrate was responsible for harmony in the district under his authority, harmony not just of the human sphere but of the relationship between humans and the natural and spiritual worlds as well. Thus his function in making offerings to spirits is crucial in bringing about harmony, yet this is scanted in most Western language discussions of the magistrate's role. For example, in Tungtsu Ch'ü's otherwise reliable compendium, *Local Government in China under the Ch'ing*, less than three pages (1962: 164–66) are devoted to "Ceremonial Observances."

On a popular level, the eminent Sinologist and Netherlands diplomat, Robert Hans van Gulik, after completing a major work on traditional Chinese jurisprudence (1956), as a hobby, wrote a series of well received detective novels in a semi-Chinese literary style based on an actual official, Di Renjie (629–700), but set in the Ming period rather than the Tang. He intended the novels to serve as a popular introduction to traditional Chinese culture, and I have so used them in an undergraduate course. In an extended "Postscript" to the first of these novels, he provided a background to the period and its literature. In discussing the district magistrate, he points out that "The magistrate's duties are manifold," and then lists a number. Conspicuously absent from this list are the magistrate's ritual duties. He continues, "Since the magistrate thus supervises practically every phase of the daily life of the people, he is commonly referred to as the 'father-and-mother official'" (1958: 282), seemingly ignoring that religion was a major aspect of the life of the people. It is to be noted, however, that in the novel, after the successful conclusion of a serious difficulty, the magistrate does offer incense at the City God, Civil, and Martial temples. But the description is of small scale personal offerings, rather than, as it would have been, large scale rituals on behalf of the entire district (207–208). That is, van Gulik understands Chinese Religion from the Western perspective of being personal rather than public and social as is Chinese state religion.

A major reason for ignoring or slighting the ritual role of the district magistrate by many scholars is the orientation toward religion of Western Sinologists or of Chinese scholars who received a Western education. Christian missionaries tended to disparage Chinese Religion as crass superstition rather than a legitimate religion. Chinese scholars educated in the West tended to accept this viewpoint whether or not they were Christian. Thus, they tended to assume that the literati officials would have considered Chinese Religion beneath them, as these Western-oriented scholars themselves did.

On the other hand, in the first half of the twentieth century, some major Western Sinologists were influenced by secular humanism (as were my own teachers in the mid-twentieth century). They admired the Chinese *rujia* ("Confucian") tradition and presumed that the Chinese intelligentsia had the same non-theistic understanding that they did. Those scholars tended to assume, for example, that Kongzi (Confucius) was agnostic (see Chapter 4 for a refutation based on a close reading of the text), seemingly ignoring his educational focus on the sincere performance of religious rituals. A substantial part of the Classics, reconstituted in the Han period with an implied connection to Kongzi, are works on these rituals.

C. K. Yang pointed to the fallacy of this viewpoint for which he provided both a Western and a Chinese example. He quotes Max Weber's statement that "the ritual was gradually emptied of all emotional elements and finally became equated with mere social convention. This was the work of the cultured stratum of intellectuals who left entirely aside the typical religious needs of the masses" and Hu Shi's statement that "the sacrifices are mere formalistic ceremonies without serious realistic significance" (1967: 178–79). We shall return to Yang's critique of these views later.

Although I had long been dissuaded from this understanding with regard to family and clan spirits, I had bought into this viewpoint with regard to the magistrate's ritual role, which I also had thought to be minor. In the spring of 2012, a visit to Pingyao in Shanxi Province, a former district capital little changed from the nineteenth century and with unusually minimal damage from the Cultural Revolution, shattered this assumption. The city now functions as a UNESCO World Heritage Site and is visited by large numbers of Chinese tourists.

In Pingyao, different from elsewhere in China, the yamen (the district government offices and magistrate's residence), the City God Temple (or *chenghuang shen* "God of Walls and Moats" Temple) and the *wenmiao* (Civil Temple, sometimes called the Temple to the First Teacher [Kongzi]) are still relatively complete. Inside the yamen, to my surprise, there were a number of temples, including two complete temple structures with the typical facing performance stages: one to the Earth deity as the deity of the locale and one to exemplary officials. This along with a placard that listed the magistrate's many religious duties, which were numerous, fostered my interest in this topic.

The magistrate's local religious duties began when he entered his new district capital and took primacy over his judicial and revenue responsibilities. When a magistrate arrives at his new post, before entering the yamen, he is expected to perform the *zhaisu* ("fast and overnight stay") ritual at the City God Temple, which includes offering incense and making an oath regarding the fulfillment of his duties. After this, he can move with his retinue into the yamen residence. On the day he takes office, wearing his official robes, the magistrate again goes to the City God Temple to make a formal offering of meat and spirit money. Afterward, the details varying from one local to another, the magistrate makes offerings to the inner quarters gate deity, the kitchen deity, and so forth. Only then does he take up his administrative duties.

Within three days after taking office, the magistrate makes a formal offering at the Civil Temple (the compliment to the Military Temple which houses Guangong, the martial deity, often in the nearby local garrison). Afterward, he goes to the examination hall within the temple grounds to greet the education officials and to ceremonially test the readiness of those qualified for the next civil service examination (Huang 1984: 94–7, 104).

The magistrate went to the Civil and City God Temples to fulfill his priestly duties a number of times throughout the year. Twice a month the magistrate offered incense to Kongzi at the Civil Temple. Complete offerings were made to Kongzi at the Civil Temple in the spring and autumn (second and eighth months according to the lunar calendar) and on Kongzi's birthday (technically since Kongzi is not a deity, the offering preferably is made by a descendant of Kongzi assisted by the magistrate); all the literati in the district were expected to attend the latter ritual. These offerings were complex and required considerable preparation.

The magistrate, as a representative of the central government and of the people of the district, was expected to offer sincere prayers to the City God whenever there were natural difficulties (drought, floods, etc.) or other problems (bandits, epidemics, etc.). He was also to make offerings at other local temples. Offerings at suburban outdoor altars were made to the Wind-Rain-Thunder-Lightening spirit, the Earth-Grain deity, and to the dead not cared for by families for various reasons, and to the mountains and rivers in his district. He also made offerings to various worthies noted in the history of the district (Huang 1984: 511–17, 623).

The above lists the basic priestly functions of the magistrate in the Ming period, reflecting those of earlier periods. During the last dynasty, the Qing, a Manchurian regime, there were far more, as the magistrate was expected to make offerings to a greater range of deities, especially as many popular deities had been co-opted by the government and provided official titles. In Pingyao, in addition to the above, the magistrate was to make offerings to the horse deity, to Guandi, and to the Jade Emperor, the latter presumably at the Daoist temple in the city (most major cities had a Daoist temple within the walls and at least one Buddhist monastery outside the walls).

The two complete temple complexes within the Pingyao yamen would also have required full ritual offerings: one to Houtu, the Lord of Earth as the deity of the locale, and at the Cuohou Temple (the Marquis of Hou or Xiao Ho). Xiao Ho (died BCE 193) was the prime minister of the first emperor of the Han dynasty, which he helped to establish. He is renowned more for his exemplary administration than as a scholar; thus, he was a role model for the magistrate. That temple complex included wings dedicated to other noted officials of the distant past. The yamen also had a temple to the Fox Deity, of importance in Manchuria and northern China, above the magistrate's residence, where the official seal was stored.

The list of temples and altars to which the magistrate made offerings, some twice a month, indicates that a substantial amount of the magistrate's time was taken up by these rituals. The sometimes complex preliminary preparations also involved a considerable amount of time. Simply based on the expenditure of time and effort, the religious ritual obligations of the magistrate were as least as important as his administrative, judicial, educational, and tax collection functions. The magistrates were fully the chief priests of their districts, as the governors were the chief priests of the provinces, and the emperor and his consort were the chief priests of the empire, indeed, of the world, China being "the pivot of the Four Quarters," the Central State (*zhongguo*).

The assumption by scholars that the magistrate's religious role was minimal or that the literati as magistrates did not engage in the ritual offerings with sincerity is contradicted by this data, as well as the vast Chinese literature on the function of ritual and the importance of sincerity in carrying out these offerings. Throughout Chinese history, sacrificial offerings, the physical manifestation of reciprocity to all facets of the spirit realm and nature, was the key to social cohesion at all levels, including government. The *Liji*, one of the three books on ritual of the Chinese Classics, well over two millennia in age, clearly states:

> Of all the ways of governing people, none is more pressing than ritual; of the five strands of ritual, none is more important than the sacrificial offerings. (Jitung chap.) [Translations for which a translator is not named are my own.]

The logograph translated as "ritual," *li*, consists of the sign for spirits next to a pictograph of a filled offering vessel. *Li* originally meant offering rituals; its use for other forms of ritual is secondary to its religious usage. The logograph translated as "sacrificial offering," *ji*, has the sign for spirits originally next to a pictograph of a hand proffering meat. The common translation of "sacrifice" is misleading as it tends to be understood in the West with the Biblical understanding, which focuses on the killing of animals and a burnt offering. In general, Chinese offerings to kin are of a multicourse cooked banquet with wine, which is eaten by the living members of the family after the ancestral spirits are satiated. Offerings to non-kin spirits are of prepared but uncooked food and wine; this food is then cooked and shared by the living.

The role of the magistrate was to represent the emperor at the local level. His priestly role was that of a surrogate for the emperor, the chief priest of the empire, and his religious duties were similar to that of the emperor. For the emperor not only made major offerings at the altar to Sky, Earth and the many other altars in the capital on special days, but his daily religious roles took up much of his time. In the *Qingdai qiju xhuce* (Daily Life Register of the Qing Dynasty), we find "In the evening [7:00–9:00 PM Western time equivalent], the emperor made offerings to the spirit realm." A commentary provides details for the first Qing emperor:

> [The first Manchurian] Emperor Shunzi [reigned 1643–1662] drew up a daily schedule for making offerings, both in the morning and the evening, to the spirit realm. In the morning, the emperor made offerings to Sakyamuni [with regard to Tibet as a major part of the empire] and the tablet to General Guan [a Chinese deity adopted by the Manchu emperors]. In the evening, he made offerings to Mongolian deities [the Mongol tribes were an important ally in

the establishment of the Manchurian Empire] and to the tablet of the founding goddess of the Aixinjueluo clan [the Manchu imperial clan].

While the deities reflect those of the ruling Manchurian clan, especially at the time of the establishment of the Manchurian Empire, the daily religious life of a Chinese magistrate was not very different for at least the last thousand years.

C. K. Yang countered Hu Shi's viewpoint quoted at the beginning of this chapter and similar views of others with the following conclusion:

> The "ceremonial formality" or "cultural vestige" view implies this assumption: Chinese ethiopolitical life might have been carried on without such cults and their sacrifices. . . . But the important fact remains that such a situation never occurred and that the ethiopolitical cults, with their temples, their sacrifices, and their mythological lore, were an integral part of the political life up until the Communist regime. This historical fact can be intelligently interpreted on one ground: the cults were significant socioreligious realities founded on their active ethiopolitical functions. (Yang 1967: 179)

The tendency to deny "this historical fact" as outlined in the preceding quotation arises from the nature of religious studies. As previously noted, comparative religion originates in Christian culture as part of the training of missionaries; hence, as delineated in Chapter 3, modern Christianity has been utilized as the model for religion in general, exemplified by dictionary definitions which focus on faith in the Christian theological sense and assume religion to be the opposite of secular. The understanding that state and religion are separable was a feature of very early Christianity, which considered unimportant family and state as it expected the imminent end of this world. But when the state decided that Christianity could be a unifying factor in reestablishing the Roman Empire, beginning with Constantine, the two became inseparable, as they are in virtually all other, save diaspora, traditions. Only with revolutions that sought to end imperial state control with its religious element, as with the American, French, and Russian revolutions, do we find a nominal separation of Christianity and the state. The inseparability of state and religion, as culture and religion, is the norm in virtually all premodern traditions.

Originally, the distinction between "religious" and "secular" in Christianity was of the two types of Roman Catholic priests following the development of formal monasticism with its special vows and regulations. Thus monk-priests who follow the monastic regulations are termed "religious" priests, conforming to the possible derivation of "religion" from the Latin *religāre* ("to bind"), while non-monastic priests are termed "secular" priests. This is a distinction which continues in the Church today. Thus, in the original use of the contrasting terms, both were within the realm of religion.

In the Chinese tradition, the primary offering rituals directed toward the dead of the family and clan bound the family together, while the state offering rituals based on the model of the clan rituals bound those who governed and those who were governed together, and the village, guild and urban neighborhood offering rituals bound non-related groups of people together. Hence, the distinction between religious and secular and between religion and the state has no meaning in the Chinese context.

Daniel Overmyer expresses this relationship between regulation and rituals in China as the same whether these are social or religious rituals:

> Regulation of what we call religious activities is simply a subset of the larger pattern, part of a continuum of social behavior, not a separate category. In this context, what I call religious rituals are ritual transactions with non-human spiritual entities, direct attempts to renew reciprocal relationship with superhuman and natural powers. (1989: 193)

My only caveat is that I would make the religious activities primary and other patterns subsets.

Similarly, there is a continuum between the family religious rituals and the civic religious rituals. A. R. Zito expresses this relationship in a most interesting and illuminating way:

> In the homologies between sons and magistrates, filial sacrifice and magisterial participation in popular ritual, the oft-assumed parallel between the Chinese family and the state was socially enacted and culturally constituted. The "centering" of a world of demons, gods, and humans through the person of a magistrate who both governed and submitted to governance simultaneously controlled the inferior, honored the superior, and gave paradoxical place to the son/magistrate/human, whose enactment of li [ritual] created the present out of the past. (1987: 366)

The magistrate's most important priestly functions took place in the City God Temple. In this regard, there is a close paralleling between the magistrate and the City God. Stephan Feuchtwang has put this quite succinctly:

> He [the City God] was thought to be the otherworld (*yin*) equivalent of the chief of the administrative capital, the this-worldly (*yang*) ruler. . . . The local administrator was the emperor's delegate to the people. The City God, as his *yin* complement, was Heaven's [*tian*, implying *tiandi*, Sky-Earth's] delegate to the people and to their dead. (1978: 123–29)

Mary Szto, a professor of law, writes similarly on the relationship of the City God and government from her own disciplinary perspective:

> City Gods played a critical role in the priesthood of government officials and the blending of ritual and law. City Gods were appointed by the Imperial government to partner with living magistrates. They were usually spirits of deceased virtuous officials. (2011: 3)

In this regard, Zito provides a historical example of a magistrate calling upon a City God to resolve a tricky judicial case—with success (1987: 335).

The role of the local official with regard to the City God is not just of the past. For the last several decades, Chinese Religion had been undergoing an ever increasing revival; more recently, there has been a growing interest in City God temples. In 2010, the mayor and deputy mayor of Guangzhou officiated at the opening ritual of the City God Temple, which had been refurbished at a cost of US$3,000,000. City officials have also been reported as praying to the City God to end corruption in the construction industry (*Statesman* 2010). In 2011, the mayor of Haimen city in responding to a letter questioning the need for spending

Figure 21 Nowadays, the old state temples serve as local temples. At the rear of the "City God" Temple in Zhengzhou, there is a full-size diorama of the City God relaxing on a bed with his wife sitting by his side.

money to refurbish the City God Temple, gave "to satisfy the people's religious needs" as one of the reasons (haimen.gov.cn). In 2012, the mayor of Taipei in Taiwan went to the City God Temple to offer incense and pray for protection and beneficial rain (fun.taipei.gov.tw). These are but a few recent instances of mayors beginning to take up the traditional magistrate's relationship with the City God. In the run-up to the recent municipal elections in Taiwan, candidates running in the legislative by-election for Taipei's second electoral district prayed for success at the local City God temple (*Focus Taiwan* 2018, 2019).

These local examples reflect events taking place on the national level, as officials are slowly taking up the traditional role of the head of state as intercessor on behalf of the people with the spirit realm. In 2009, the honorary chairman of the Nationalist Party, Lien Chan, and his wife were part of a thirty-five-member delegation from Taiwan to join with Mainland government officials in ceremonies at Huangdi's Mausoleum on Qiaoshan in Shaanxi Province on the day of Qingming, the traditional day to visit ancestral graves (http://english.people.com.cn/90001/90783/91300/6630239.html). Huangdi is honored as the grand ancestor of the Chinese people (as distinct from deities, such as Nüwa and Fuxi, who are understood to be the parents of all humans). Lien is reported to have said, "The Tomb Sweeping Day [*qingming*] is a time for Chinese to trace their origins and pay respects to their ancestors." The day previous, the president of Taiwan, Ma Ying-jeou, led a ceremony directed toward Huangdi at the Martyr's Shrine in Taipei. All these ceremonies have since continued.

Conclusion

Thus the magistrate was not only a priest in the sense of performing rituals on behalf of his district but, more importantly, was also a priest in being the intermediary between the people of his district and the natural and spirit realms, carrying out this role via ritual offerings and ritually dialoguing with the spirits during times of natural and other disasters. The goal of his actions was to bring about harmony, the primary sociocultural value, harmony not just within society, but harmony in the cosmos itself.

The relationship between ritual and harmony was articulated in China's earliest philosophical writing. In the *Lunyu* ("Analects of Confucius"), we find:

> Of the things brought about by the rites, harmony is the most valuable. Of the ways of the Former Kings, this is the most beautiful, and is followed alike in

matters great and small, yet this will not always work: to aim always at harmony
without regulating it by the rites simply because one knows only about harmony
will not, in fact, work. (I,12; trans.by Lau 1979: 61)

Harmony can only be established through properly regulated rituals, thus
bringing us back to the original meaning of "religion." Hence, the primary
role of the magistrate was as a priest, carrying out rituals as the emperor's
local surrogate.

If full harmony were to be achieved—a virtually impossible ideal—then there
would be no need for the magistrate's judicial functions, for there would be
no crime or public disorder, let alone natural disasters. The ideal government
in China was no government at all; there would be no need for it. But there
would remain a need for this harmony to be maintained, which on the local level
was through the ritual relationship between the two imperial appointees, the
magistrate and the City God. Hence, the magistrate carried out at the local level
the state religion which was synonymous with the government and essential for
the harmony of the district he governed.

When presenting an early form of this chapter to receptive Chinese colleagues
in Beijing in 2014, I was admonished by one faculty member to remember that
the Chinese Communist Party is officially atheistic and party members are not
allowed to belong to a religion, meaning a religious institution. Chinese Religion
per se is not institutionalized and thus not officially considered a religion; it is
deemed a "folk" or "popular" cultural practice, thus avoiding a dilemma for
members of the Party and the Party itself. So as not to embarrass my Chinese
friends, I will conclude by accepting that the present government is not a
religious institution per se, even though it increasingly resembles one from a
comparative perspective.

7

Freedom of Religion in China: In the Past and Under the Chinese Communist Party

Introduction

I grew up in Baltimore and my seventh grade civics teacher proudly pointed out that Maryland had the earliest religious freedom law: the Maryland Toleration Act of 1649. Cecil Calvert, Lord Baltimore, sought a refuge for Catholics in establishing the Maryland colony. The Act provided freedom of worship for all Christians, but demanded the death sentence for denying the divinity of Jesus. The majority of the students in the class were Jewish, and somehow the teacher was oblivious of the fact that the act she was praising called for the execution of most of the students in her class!

"Religious freedom," to varying degrees but usually only when applied to Christianity, devolves from the American and French revolutions. The US government presently uses the term as a tool to critique governments to which it is opposed but does not provide full religious freedom to all of its citizens. The present Canadian government, which generally follows the US lead in this regard, is even more lacking in providing religious freedom to Native traditionalists. What the complaint regarding a country not having religious freedom often means is that Western-controlled forms of Christianity, often fundamentalist, are not free to proselytize.

Suppression of religious institutions and individual freedom of religion

If we understand the traditional Chinese state to be a religious institution, then the relationship between state and religion in China is clarified. Three thousand years ago, when the ruling clan of what became the Zhou kingdom conquered the Shang kingdom, their first act was to pull down the Shang clan temple, thus destroying their spiritual power as well. The justification for kingship and, a thousand years later, imperial rule was that the ruler was *Tianzu* (Child of Sky), meaning the immediate descendant of the most powerful conglomerate of clan spirits in the Sky, most powerful because they are the deceased rulers or founders of the most powerful clan. Thus, he, the *Yiren* (the "One Person" meaning the emperor—it is lonely at the top), was the only one who could make offerings to Sky and thus mediate between humans and the superior ancestral spiritual power located in the Sky. Moreover, only the One Person could make offerings to Sky-Earth, the cosmic forces that generated all existence on behalf of humans everywhere; for others to do so was treason.

When the Ming dynasty moved the capital from Nanjing to Beijing in the early fifteenth century, they constructed a series of imperial altars. On one side of the gate to the palace was the imperial clan temple, and on the other side was the altar to soil and grain, following the prescriptions of the millennia-old classics of ritual. At a moderate distance from the palace in each of the four directions were the altars to Sky, Earth, Sun, and Moon. There were several other imperial altars as well (see Meyer 1991). Only the emperor could make offerings at these altars, and this function as chief priest of Chinese civilization, if not the world itself, China being the Middle Kingdom (Zhongguo), theoretically justified his political authority.

The state being a religious institution, the supremacy of the state could be best challenged by new competing religious institutions. When the first successful Chinese empire, the Han, was collapsing after nearly 400 years in the second century, it was challenged by an increasingly popular religio-political movement and its army, the Five Pecks of Rice, perhaps indirectly influenced by the then recent entry of Buddhism into China. Their religious text was the *Taiping Jing*, the term *"Taiping"* ("Great Peace") later taken for the name of the indigenous Christian religio-political movement of the mid-nineteenth century. The Five Pecks of Rice revolt was put down after much struggle, but the Han dynasty was so weakened that the general in charge of the Han army was able to put his son on the throne as the emperor of a new dynasty, leading to the breakup of the empire. The defeated, now depoliticized, Five Pecks of Rice movement became the seed of the Daoist churches.

In the interregnum between the Han and the second major Chinese empire, the Tang, Buddhism developed into a significant aspect of Chinese culture, offering institutional stability in periods of political chaos. Due to accepting gifts of land and money for spiritual merit, Buddhism became a substantial economic power; monasteries began owning large tracts of tax-exempt land, and there were increasingly large numbers of non-tax paying monks and nuns. The concentration of non-taxable wealth and persons in Buddhist institutions at times threatened the economic viability of the state, and there were several crackdowns on their power. Finally, in the ninth century, the Tang government carried out a major suppression of Buddhist institutions, but there was no concern with the religious practices of individuals (see Chapter 8 for details). After the monasteries lost their wealth, only Sinicized modes of Buddhism remained viable. Buddhism lost its popularity in China, never regaining it until the twentieth century, when it became perceived as a favorable indigenous parallel to the disliked foreign Christianity.

When the Mongols added China to their empire in the thirteenth century, a number of martial Buddhist religio-political movements arose against them. A century later, the first Ming emperor arose from one of them and succeeded in defeating the Mongol army. When the Manchurians later conquered the weakened Ming dynasty in the seventeenth century, anti-foreign Buddhist religio-political movements arose again. In the mid-nineteenth century, an indigenous Christian movement, the Taiping, was able to raise a vast army and conquered much of China. The Manchu regime, considerably weakened by internal corruption and European aggression, particularly the first Opium War, only succeeded in putting down the revolt with the help of European armies, the combined armies led by an English general, "Chinese" Gordon. The Europeans considered the leader of the Taiping, who understood himself to be the new Messiah, being the younger brother of Jesus, anathema, and wanted a weak Manchu government to continue rather than be replaced by a new, strong regime (see Paper 1995b: chap. 9). The Chinese empire collapsed into chaos a half-century later, to be finally united when the communists won the civil war in 1949.

Thus, the political history of China can be seen in large part as a history of competing religio-political institutions. China is constantly portrayed in the West, particularly by the United States, as a Marxist state that persecutes religion and accordingly violates human rights. Yet China has no history of religious persecution. Indeed, Chinese governments have patronized other religious institutions so long as these institutions accepted the sovereignty of the state. During the Han dynasty, the state supported the building of Buddhist monasteries; Buddhist, Daoist, and Nestorian Christian monasteries during the Tang; and Jewish synagogues during the post-Song and Ming periods. During the extreme destruction of the Cultural Revolution, everything old was subject to destruction— religious building and artifacts were not especially singled out. The inclination of

Chinese governments to co-opt religious modes into its own bailiwick is evident in that the government in Taiwan urged spirit mediums to create a registered religious institution after the end of martial law in 1987 (see Chapter 5).

Today, this long-lived Chinese policy continues. There is complete religious freedom, but all institutions, including religious ones, must be indigenous, even if of foreign origination, and registered with the state. The two-millennia-long history of religio-political institutions competing with the state, as well as Christian missionaries preceding Western colonialism (see following chapter), is hardly forgotten. The cries of violation of human rights through the denial of religious freedom by anti-Chinese Western governments hinge on this point. Of the usual examples, all involve the refusal to comply with government regulations and/or are foreign-controlled institutions seeking to replace the Chinese government.

The Chinese government long recognized a Catholic Church registered with the government but has not recognized a Catholic Church subject to the Vatican, which is officially a sovereign foreign state. The Chinese learned the hard way— the treaties following the "Opium Wars"—that foreign-controlled religions are the "shock troops" of imperialist expansion. (Japan came to understand this in the seventeenth century and cut off almost all contact with the West.) This attitude toward a Vatican-controlled religion was initially set when the Vatican contradicted a decision of the Chinese emperor in the eighteenth century with regard to the century-long Rites Controversy. The emperor gave missionaries the choice of agreeing with him (he accepted the Jesuit understanding) or the Vatican (which sided with the Dominicans and Franciscans), which meant the virtual end, until the Opium Wars, of Christianity in China. In more recent times, Vatican II reinstated the Jesuit position with regard to Chinese Catholics making offerings to their ancestors. But this situation is coming to an end as in late 2018 an accommodation was worked out with the Vatican regarding a shared control of the Church in China between the Chinese government and the Vatican (see Chapter 8 for details).

The treaties following the Opium Wars gave considerable latitude to Christian missionaries. In particular, the French language version of the treaty following the second war gave extraterritoriality not only to missionaries but to their Chinese converts as well, meaning that Chinese Christians could enact the most heinous of crimes and could not be prosecuted by the Chinese government. To support missionaries and their converts, US gunboats patrolled over a thousand kilometers of the Yangze River. (An excellent depiction of this situation will be found in the 1966 film, "The Sand Pebbles," based on a novel written by a former

US sailor on one of the American Yangze River gunboats.) Hatred of missionaries and converts reached such a degree that many were killed during the so-called "Boxer" movement in the late nineteenth century. When the present regime began, among its first acts was to deport most Christian missionaries (some medical and other non-proselytizing missionaries were encouraged to stay).

Thus the Chinese government is highly suspicious of Protestant churches influenced by fundamentalist evangelical American churches to break the law. The "house churches" are fundamentalist Protestant (often Pentecostal) churches that deliberately refuse to register, meaning that they do not recognize the legitimacy of the Chinese state. Their suppression is not based on the religious aspects but the non-compliance aspect, as well as their practice of secret membership and meeting places. An institution that demands secrecy is ipso facto assumed to be seditious in China, an understanding based on two thousand years of experience with secret religio-political movements. There are, of course, a large number of registered Protestant churches, which are supported by the government.

The Tibet issue is not a matter of religious freedom but of who governs Tibet and a large part of China. Tibet has a long history of being sequentially controlled by Mongolia, Manchuria, and China as an autonomous region or of controlling China. Tibet conquered much of China in the eighth century and the government-in-exile in India claims sovereignty over a substantial part of China because of having been within the borders of the former Tibetan Empire for a very short time. The Chinese government recognizes Tibetan Buddhism under a number of Lamas (who are but abbots of monasteries), especially the Panchen Lama, but not the Dalai Lama, because he is claimed to be the theocratic ruler of most of China. I have found functioning Tibetan Buddhist temples in a number of areas of China, as well as Tibetan monks freely traveling throughout China. But those Tibetans who acknowledge the Dalai Lama as the ruler of Tibet and the majority of Chinese territory will indeed be persecuted.

The understanding in the West of the Dalai Lama as the theocratic ruler of Tibet, of a particular abbot replacing the Tibetan king, rather than as the abbot of a single monastery, was created by the British government well over a century ago in its struggle over that part of the world, especially Afghanistan, with Russia (the "Great Game"). Their purpose was to wrest Tibet from the control of China and add it to India and thus the British Empire.

In 1950, with the reunification of China, China reasserted control over Tibet, a control which had been but nominal in the previous half-century, and began the end of involuntary serfdom (the basis of Tibetan economy in which serfs farmed monastic land—for an example, see Grimshaw 1992), which challenged the authority of the monasteries over the lives of the people, save for the merchants. In 1956, the CIA fomented what is by now a well-documented revolt (see Conboy and Morrison 2002), which as expected failed. But this brought the Chinese army into Tibet, creating a military emergency in the west to balance the US-armed Taiwan in the east, then threatening to invade China, and pinning down a large force on the coast. This forced China into a military confrontation on two fronts. A second revolt in 1959 led to the formation in India of a Tibetan government-in-exile supported by the United States, the young Dalai Lama having been unwillingly led out of China, which has since been used for extensive anti-Chinese propaganda.

During the Cultural Revolution, from 1966–76, Tibetan monasteries were severely trashed by Tibetan, not Chinese, youths, as local youths everywhere in China were urged to destroy everything considered non-modern, including religious buildings and artifacts. Neither Tibet nor religion was selected out. Everything old was considered evil.

A more recent Western complaint regarding religious freedom in Tibet is that monks who burned alive Han Chinese merchants in Lhasa in 2008 were arrested for murder. This is a very new interpretation of religious freedom and of Buddhist religious practices. The present Chinese government, of course, will not accept as the political ruler of an autonomous Chinese region a person chosen by assumed transmigration from a dead person to an infant nor allow the socioeconomic structure to revert to serfdom.

From personal experience, in all of my visits to China since the mid-1980s, I encountered Tibetan Buddhism flourishing unhampered. The next-to-last time I was in China, I stopped at a functioning, non-tourist Tibetan temple in Yunnan Province, near the border with Tibet. There was no evidence whatsoever of suppression, although the local non-Buddhist indigenous people were far from happy with it being there. On previous trips to China over the last quarter century, I always met some Tibetan monks in various parts of China.

The issue of the Falun Gong is a peculiar situation in the history of US-China relations. The Falun Gong, following a controversial, very minor beginning in China, in 1998 emerged full-fledged in New York, lush with funding sufficient for a large suite of offices, widely distributed free anti-China Chinese and English-language newspapers (without mention of the owner), and so forth. According to their Chinese language website in 2002, the founder, Li Hongzhi received his teachings from outer-space aliens and is a god higher than Jesus or the Buddha; he personally controls adherents' life, death, and salvation. (The website is now far more sophisticated and appears to be the same in all languages.) A major mission of Li, expressed in a 1999 interview, was to save the planet from already present alien invaders from outer space (Dowell 1999).

The Falun Gong achieved notoriety in 1999, when more than ten thousand followers on short notice completely encircled the legislature building in central Beijing in a bizarre bid for government recognition. A few months later, several provincial government buildings were similarly surrounded, with some placed under siege. Recognition in this case seemed to mean acceptance of Li as a superior being and thus the true ruler of China, a common theme in Chinese folklore. This challenge to the government for control of China, of course, led to a severe, continuing crackdown, as would a similar attempt at a coup in Western countries. In 2002, the organization took control for eight days of China's Sinosat-1 TV satellite, a task, one assumes, that could only be accomplished by the enormous technical resources of the United States's NSA ("Falun Gong . . ." 2002).

Since 1999, the organization has made many preposterous claims, including having 100 million members in China (over 10 percent of China's adult population) incarcerated for organ harvesting. The claim that anyone caught practicing *qigong* in China—an age-old tradition—is arrested is belied by the many who can be seen doing *qigong* early in the morning every day in virtually all the urban parks in China. Every Chinese I happened to have talked to in China, Taiwan, and Canada in these regards assumed that since the Falun Gong moved to the United States, the organization has been CIA sponsored for the purpose of destabilizing China (this is an anecdotal, not a statistical or sociological, finding).

Finally, the situation with regard to the Uyghurs (the meaning and application of the name is controversial) has nothing to do with Islam per se. The Manchu empire attached the Uyghurs by force to their empire in the eighteenth century, and they have been struggling for independence ever since. The Nationalist government, followed by the Communist government, maintained the territory of the Manchu empire, thus inheriting the problem of an ethnic group unwilling to be a part of China. Since the province where they live, Xinjiang, is rich in oil and other resources, they have little chance in achieving independence and have resorted to terrorism. Apparently, some have been trained in terrorist training camps in Afghanistan and elsewhere, and being a Turkic people, they are receiving support from Turkic nations.

Chinese Muslim communities have a long history in China. Chinese Muslims were well integrated into Chinese culture a thousand years ago, and many became high officials and military leaders. The famous admiral Cheng Ho, who led huge maritime expeditions around much of the world in the fifteenth century, was a Muslim. The situation with Uyghur Muslims, their country attached to China as part of the Manchu Empire, is quite different. They have always resisted being part of China and are now supported by foreign Islamist movements. China understands this situation as one of an Uyghur militant separatist movement and terrorism rather than a matter of religion; Islam itself is officially recognized and considered a part of the Chinese cultural matrix. There are functioning mosques in virtually every Chinese city, along with Muslim schools, and Muslim (halal) restaurants are everywhere.

The suppression of Uighur terrorism is invariably interpreted in the Western press as religious suppression of Islam. Uighur terrorists have hacked people to death in Chinese railroad stations and trains. When I last traveled in China, extensively by train, those entering major railroad stations were subjected to personal and x-ray baggage searches similar to those at airports, due to fear of Uyghur terrorism. On November 10, 2009, the CBC announced on its website that "China has executed nine men for participating in ethnic rioting in the country's northwest that left almost 200 people dead." But they were not convicted for rioting, rather they were convicted for mass murder.

When I first visited China in 1983 and 1986, at the end of the Cultural Revolution, people were unsure if the government's negative attitude toward religion and other Chinese traditions, which reached its height during the Cultural Revolution, had genuinely changed and were reticent to speak to foreigners. The household altars that I saw were hidden in back rooms rather than in the main room as is traditional in older style houses. The few temples that had been refurbished after the rampant destruction of everything "old" were done so for Japanese tourism, although groups on pilgrimages were evident—youths watched those middle-aged and older pilgrims praying at these "tourist" sites with great curiosity—and Buddhist and Daoist monks and nuns were returning from having been laicized. When I returned in 1992, the situation was vastly different. People were eager to talk about religion, stores selling religious paraphernalia did so openly, and temples were rapidly being refurbished. Christian churches and Muslim mosques were also flourishing. On subsequent visits to the present, I found throughout China large numbers of youths making offerings at temples of all sorts, family altars openly displayed, and so forth.

Under Xi Jinping, the situation regarding religious institutions has been clarified and regularized. According to a report in *Reuters World News* on September 7, 2017, "China's cabinet on Thursday passed new rules to regulate religion to bolster national security, fight extremism and restrict faith practiced outside organizations approved by the state." The new law (http://www.gov.cn/z hengce/content/2017-09/07/content_5223282.htm) is to replace the one of 2005. The focus of the regulations is that the management of religious affairs should adhere to the principles of protecting "legitimate religious activities, curbing and preventing extreme practices and resisting infiltration."

Wang Zuoan, the director of the State Administration for Religious Affairs, was quoted in the *Global Times* (a Chinese government publication) in July 2017 saying that religion in China needed to be "Sinicized" and for religious groups to focus on parts that are "beneficial to social harmony and development.... Foreign forces have used religion to infiltrate China, and extremism and illegal religious activities are spreading in some places, which have threatened national security and social stability." The new law stresses the need to protect China's national security against threats from religious groups. President Xi Jinping has been reported as emphasizing the need to guard against foreign infiltration through religion and to prevent the spread of "extremist" ideology, while being tolerant of officially recognized religions that he sees as a means to ameliorate social ills.

The new law, which came into effect on February 2, 2018, places new oversight on online discussion of religious matters, on religious gatherings, the financing of religious groups and the construction of religious buildings, etc. It increases existing restrictions on unregistered religious groups and includes explicit bans on foreigners teaching about religion or encouraging Chinese to go abroad to take part in religious (or terrorist) training or meetings. The new law includes provisions on the raising of religious funds, and donations from foreign groups or individuals are banned.

The law is particularly aimed at three developments. The first is the unregistered "house churches," which are financed and supported by evangelical missionaries from North America. Second is the spread of Salafism among Chinese Muslims throughout China, which I have witnessed, supported by Gulf states, including the building of new mosques in the Arabian style rather than Chinese architecture as in the past. Third is the infiltration of extremists in encouraging an Uyghur struggle for independence through violence, including terrorist attacks in railroad stations and on trains throughout China. The incarceration of Uyghurs in "reeducation" camps is being done as a matter of state security, not religion; throughout my travels through China to the present, I have found Islam freely practiced everywhere. Caught up in this crackdown have been efforts to help the Chinese Jews revitalize their Judaism (see Chapter 9), but on non-Chinese Jewish models by Jewish-American missionaries and foreign funds.

By the end of 2018, unregistered churches, including huge and expensive structures (one reportedly having the capacity of fifty thousand congregants), have been torn down for having been erected illegally, and illegal religious leaders have been arrested. As well, a Chinese-American Jew actively teaching the Ashkenazi version of Judaism to the Chinese Jews in Kaifeng and publicizing to the foreign press a Jewish ceremony in the foreign (Ashkenazi) mode held in a hotel for the remnant Chinese Jewish population in Kaifeng has been deported as a foreign missionary. (I had previously tried to warn his US sponsors that this would likely happen if his blatant missionary activities continued.)

The concern about sedition in the above quotations should be understood as genuine. All of this suppression has to be understood in the context of Chinese history, since virtually all regime changes have been due to revolts by religious movements. Given that the unregistered evangelical churches have tended to speak against the Communist Party and the government, were often led by foreign missionaries, and were maintained by foreign funds, seemingly supported by American intelligence agencies, the assumption of sedition can be readily understood. The same can be said, with different foreign influences, with regard to Uyghur terrorism, and the very recent turning of some mosques away from being within Chinese Islam to focus on Saudi Arabia and Arab culture. The Falun Gong openly calls for the overthrow of the Chinese government, and the American-supported Tibetan government-in-exile in northern India demands control over much of China. One can take the viewpoint that the past does not affect the present (not my view, of course), but Chinese culture is the most historically oriented culture in the world; Chinese historical writing is among the earliest in the world; and historical documents and substantial works on history were a major part of traditional education. A Westerner may ignore history, but the Chinese do not.

In summary, state and religion have always been coterminous in China. Save for the excesses of the period leading up to and during the Cultural Revolution, religious freedom for individuals was never an issue. Chinese Religion is not a matter of belief, since having parents and grandparents is a matter of knowing rather than belief in the illogical (following the Church Father Tertullian's understanding of belief). Thus, Chinese Religion is not creedal as is Christianity and there is no expectation of belief, let alone adhering to a creed. Chinese Pure Land Buddhism contains belief—belief in the saving power of Amida Bodhisattva—but this belief is neither demanded nor required. Hence, the concept of the imposition of a religious belief, as it exists in Christianity, or adherence to a belief statement, as found in Islam, is not an aspect of Chinese Religion or culture.

During the Cultural Revolution, there was a policy to destroy family-centered religion and replace it with adherence to society as a whole, reminiscent of the concept of *boai* (universal love) promulgated by Mozi 2,400 years ago. The concept even then was generally understood as unworkable; society as a whole was too amorphous to receive the same attachment from individuals as did family and clan. Similarly, after the Cultural Revolution, the government realized that Familism could not be replaced by devotion to society as a whole and that the attempted destruction of family and local religion led to a serious moral vacuum with far-reaching consequences. Since then, there has been little or no concern with individual thinking or practices in this regard; traditional religion is slowly resurgent with government approval, as it is "diffused" (non-institutional), and religious institutions are flourishing, so long as they are registered. But any institution, especially religious ones, that flouts government regulations and/or is controlled by foreign institutions or governments, continues to be considered illegitimate and a threat to public order and is, accordingly, quashed. As has been the case throughout history, the government has little concern over individual religious thinking.

In my travels China over the past decades, I have lived in and visited many Buddhist monasteries, including those of Tibetan Buddhism. I have been in Daoist monasteries and been close to several Daoist monks and priests. I am familiar with the practices of Chinese Religion by those families I have been close to, either by relationship or friendship. I have been in many temples of various sorts, as well as mosques, where I have discussed my research with imams. Never once have I witnessed any government concern over religious belief or adherence. And I have been invited to openly discuss the views on religion expressed in this book in public lectures at Beijing universities.

Because Chinese are acculturated to understand Familism (*xiao*) to be the foundation of Chinese culture and society, and the governments in Mainland China and Taiwan affirm this, there is no concern about alternative religious understandings. This is because these alternative understandings of long-standing in China are understood to be adjunct and complimentary to Familism; they are perceived as possibly interesting but not a threat. Chinese culture has a long history of assimilation and synthesis to better the goal of harmony; hence, some alternative religions are gathered into a homogeneous yet complex religious construct. Thus, the "*san jiao* (Three Teachings) are one" has been reiterated over the centuries. Given these attitudes, in a culture without a concept of a single truth, it is hardly surprising, in contrast to Western Christian culture, that religious freedom, leaving out concerns over sedition, is the norm.

As a Jew, I have suffered from many forms of discrimination in the United States, especially in the 1940s through the early 1970s. And I still find animosity, sometimes vicious, against myself for being a Jew by some in the United States and Canada. But I have never felt anything of that sort in China.

It is most ironic that the issue of religious freedom is used by the West to attack China given that the West has been far more flagrant in persecuting people and groups for their religious beliefs, or lack thereof. Even in the twentieth century, following centuries of religious wars between Christian factions, as well as the Crusades against Muslims (and Jews in the First Crusade), Jews in Russia and the countries it controlled suffered from pogroms in which Jews were murdered and raped; Jews could not live in Franco-controlled Spain; and Germany slaughtered millions of Jews. Native American religions for decades were illegal in the United States and Canada. Native people were incarcerated in Canada simply for taking part in their religious rituals, specifically for giving gifts, yet Christians were not incarcerated for doing exactly the same during Christmas. As I write this, the US government limits visitation by Muslims from Muslim countries. There is no evidence that anything like this ever took place in China, save by indigenous Christians during the Taiping Movement or in response to Christian outrages during the "Boxer" movement. The West's criticism of China with regard to religious freedom seems to be more a reflection of their own tradition rather than that of China.

"Freedom of Religion" in the context of the long US conflict with China

In the December 18, 2018, "Letter of Resignation" by the secretary of defense to the American president, General Mattis writes:

> Similarly, I believe we must be resolute and unambiguous in our approach to those countries whose strategic interests are increasingly in tension with ours. It is clear that China and Russia, for example, want to shape a world consistent with their authoritarian model . . . to promote their own interests at the expense of their neighbors, America and our Allies. That is, we must use all the tools of American power to provide for the common defense.

The United States has been at war, hot and cold, with the Soviet Union/ Russia, except during the Second World War, since the 1918 Anglo-American Expeditionary Force, North Russia, invaded Russia but failed to reinstate the

Czarist regime. The US government has continuously assumed that the Chinese Communist Party is a puppet of Russia, and thus equally an enemy, and based its foreign policy on this incorrect assumption.

This understanding of "communism" everywhere being part of a Soviet plot against the U.S. continues. In a secret history of the CIA by Richard Helms, when he was director of Central intelligence, declassified in 2007, we find,

> Angleton [CIA's counterintelligence chief] believed that the Soviet Union. . . was implacable in its hostility toward the West. International Communism remained monolithic, and reports of a rift between Moscow and Peking were only part of an elaborate "disinformation campaign." (Weiner 2008: 317)

Stalin was antagonistic to the Chinese Communist Party as it developed under Mao Zedong because, following Marxist-Leninist orthodoxy, he understood that communism can only develop from a proletariat, which China did not have, being at that time an agrarian economy with slight industrialization. Mao based his communism on the peasantry in spite of the Soviet insistence that China must first industrialize and have a proletariat before it could become socialist. Hence, the Soviet Union did not substantially assist the Chinese Communist Party during the Civil War. Until very recently, China and Russia have been at odds with each other and fought several battles along their border in 1969, the border tension continuing in several areas.

The US Congress tended to perceive the civil war in China as a religious one, a war between the "Godless" Chinese Communist Party and an American Protestant–influenced Nationalist Party, led by the nominally Methodist Chiang Kai-shek. His wife, a Methodist and a symbol in the United States of an American-influenced Protestant Christian China, addressed a joint session of Congress in 1943.

Toward the end of the Second World War in the Pacific, US State Department experts on China advised their government to support the Chinese Communist Party since there was no doubt that they would win the civil war, which would follow the defeat of Japan, due to massive Nationalist Party corruption and the Communist Party support of the peasantry against rapacious landlords. From a realpolitik standpoint, the United States would be in a better position to influence China if they supported the winner of the civil war. When the Communist Party defeated the Nationalist Party, the Republican Party in the United States blamed the Democratic Party for not all-out supporting the "Christian" Nationalists, for "giving" China to godless communists; the State Department specialists were fired. Mao Zedong naively assumed that the United States would see him as a

Chinese George Washington and expected to be invited to visit Washington as a hero. When Zhou Enlai met the US secretary of state around that time he held out his hand and Dean Rusk refused to take it.

Since the entry of China into the Korean War due to General MacArthur threatening to cross the border and invade China to overthrow communism without government authorization (he was fired by President Truman after the fact), the United States has sought to militarily contain China. The United States armed and supplied military advisers to Taiwan, which then threatened to invade the mainland (posters to this effect were omnipresent when I lived there in the mid-1960s), instigated a revolt in Tibet by air-dropping arms to rebel forces, supported a Catholic government seeking to impose Christianity on Vietnam under the ruse of resisting Chinese (rather than indigenous) communism, and maintained a strict embargo. The embargo was ended by President Nixon, but other aspects continue to the present. More recently, the US government under Obama promised Japan it would militarily hold for them the Chinese islands the United States gave Japan after the war, encouraged Japan to revise its constitution to allow an aggressive military, and encouraged large procurement of modern arms from the United States presumably to be used against China.

The constant carping about the lack of freedom of religion in China is but one example of the Western false propaganda against China and the Chinese in order to present them as dangerous atheists and a threat to the West. The most egregious propaganda is the constant harping on a massacre that never happened, in order to portray the Chinese as dangerous barbarians with no regard for human life, similar to the way that Germans were portrayed during the First World War and the Japanese during the Second World War. Virtually all cultures dehumanize their enemies to justify warring against them.

In the spring of 1989, a student protest against corruption and for greater "democracy" spread among workers throughout China who were upset by the massive economic changes taking place with the shift from socialism to capitalism. Most important was bringing to an end the "iron rice bowl," meaning workers could not be fired regardless of whether they worked or not; thus, industry was burdened by highly bloated payrolls. Thus, many workers lost their jobs, and some raided armories, took weapons, and initiated an informal revolt. University students had been camping in the large Tiananmen Square in the heart of Beijing for a long period, and the government announced a crackdown to clear the Square and bring order back to the capital. On June 4, the Square was surrounded by the army. Chai Ling, a student leader, said in a filmed interview "What we are actually hoping for is bloodshed. . . . Only when the Square is awash with blood will the people of China open their eyes" (Gordon and Hinton 1995). Earlier, she stated that she and the other leaders' purpose was to "overthrow" the government by violent means. Later on the 4th, she announced to reporters that many students had been massacred in the Square, the numbers continually changing. Other student leaders also claimed to have seen hundreds die and tanks roll over people sleeping in tents. Liberal organizations the world over decried the assumed butchery, with numbers of the slaughtered given in the many thousands.

In the same documentary, a university teacher spoke of going to the soldiers and their agreeing to wait until the students left before entering the Square. The voiceover footage showing an empty Square went, "At dawn on June 4th, after occupying the Square for more than three weeks, all the remaining students and their teachers and supporters left Tiananmen Square. Tiananmen Square was empty." Not a single student was there when the tanks rolled in. Unfortunately, some students instead of going home or back to the universities apparently headed toward the sounds of fighting not far off and were wounded or killed by the crossfire. Workers had attacked the army convoys with Molotov cocktails and gunfire and the soldiers fired back. Soldiers and workers, as well as many innocent bystanders, were killed or wounded in the melee.

I had been skeptical from the start about the claim that Chinese soldiers massacred students; it made no sense given my understanding of Chinese culture, based on decades of studying Chinese values. As discussed, Chinese culture is based on *xiao*, Familism, which includes the country as a whole. Chinese troops would not fire on unarmed students; they would have pushed them out of the Square by force, but would not have killed them. (The same cannot be said with regard to American soldiers, given the killing of unarmed students at Kent State in 1970.) A couple of years later, I was with graduate students in Beijing who had been involved in the protests. I asked them if they knew the names of any students who were killed or wounded in the Square; none could think of a single name. Thus, I concluded that no one had been killed there. Some reporters interviewing students came to similar conclusions.

A recently declassified cable of June 19, 1989, from the US embassy in Beijing to various Department of State recipients contained the following statement:

> In the following narrative and chronology, the embassy attempts to set the record straight. . . . We conclude that contrary to a number of early Western press accounts . . . the PLA did not fire directly on students gathered around the Martyrs Monument on Tiananmen Square. . . . Witnesses present at the Martyrs

> Monument describe an eerie lack of action on the Square proper during the
> shooting in the streets. We have heard no accounts of soldiers firing directly
> on students crowded around the Martyrs Monument in the Square. As far as
> they could tell, no students were present in the tents which APC's rolled over as
> they entered the Square before sunrise on June 4. The several thousand students
> who remained at the monument departed the Square via the southeast corner
> beginning at about 05:00, June 4. (State Department 1989)

Hence, there can be no doubt that the US government was well aware within
two weeks after the supposed incident that no massacre took place. Yet, the
US government continues to castigate China for a fictitious massacre, and
the Canadian prime minister has said that the Canadian government cannot
sign a trade agreement with China until it apologizes for a massacre that
never occurred!

The Western mindset in general has long been antagonistic to China and
Chinese. Anger at a failed colonialism seems not to have dissipated. As a number
of studies have pointed out, colonialism requires a racist mindset, a mindset that
considers colonized people as inferior, to justify "civilizing (e.g., Christianizing)
inferior humans"—"white man's burden." When in conversation with
colleagues, I mentioned the State Department cables denying a massacre, a
professor of philosophy specializing in ethics stated that he did not care about the
cable, because he was certain that a massacre took place regardless of evidence as
"the Chinese are inhumane." Even the writers for PBS Frontline wrote in a blurb
for the documentary, "The Gate of Heavenly Peace," which explicitly denies that
a massacre took place, "the film reflects five years of meticulous research and
interviews to construct the most complete and accurate account to date of the
complex political process that eventually led to the Beijing Massacre of June 4"
(Frontline 1995).

Readers of this book may wonder about this seeming digression from an
analysis of Chinese Religion. The purpose is to point out that vilifying China
for a horrible event that never occurred, propaganda that can be proven a
prevarication, is no different from the constant carping on the lack of freedom
of religion in China. This is also false propaganda to justify hostile action against
China, whether of trade or potential war. This is not to suggest that, aside from
the fiction of lack of freedom of religion in China, there are not other aspects of
a serious lack of human rights from a modern Western perspective, particularly
with regard to local government behavior, but also with regard to freedom of
expression, freedom to receive information, freedom to criticize the Communist
Party, as well as the jailing of human rights lawyers, etc. In China, social stability

has always been considered of greater value than freedom of individual behavior and society more important than the individual, the opposite of modern Western values.

Up to the mid-seventeenth century, China was technologically the most advanced civilization in the world. For example, the maritime expansion of Portugal and Spain was dependent on Chinese navigation instruments, ship design, and Chinese mariners having long navigated the routes used by European explorers to reach Asia; similarly, Europe's ability to colonize was, in part, based on cannons first developed in China and then vastly improved in Europe. China was then the largest and most powerful country. Huge Chinese sea-going vessels traded as far as Africa. But for reasons too complex to detail here, China's intellectual development was stultified by the government beginning with the Mongol regime, its military ability was weakened due to later inept governments, its naval and merchant fleets were destroyed by the Ming government, and it was conquered first by the Manchus, then by Western naval and army forces, and finally by Japan. But that was the past; the Chinese present is different.

As China seeks to regain its place in the world—economically, scientifically, technologically, militarily, etc.—there is increasing tension between the United States, presently the most powerful country in the world which wishes to remain so, and emerging China (see US Government 2017). As I write this, the trade war created by the United States against China could shift into a military confrontation once the American president realizes that the imposed tariffs hurt the US economy more than the economy of China. The continued propaganda against China, including on the issue of freedom of religion, is a symptom of this tension. A major reason for this tension is the lack of recognition, let alone understanding, of Chinese Religion.

Familism does not teach that there is a single truth, not does it proselytize, since families are the human norm. Thus, Familism does not lead to crusades, etc. China has not expanded territorially for over a thousand years, and the previous expansions were narrow bands around the Gobi desert to make secure the overland trade route through Central Asia. It was the Manchus that expanded their empire to include Tibet and the Uyghur's homeland, but both the Republic of China and the People's Republic of China sought to maintain the Manchu empire's borders after it collapsed in the early twentieth century. The current militarization of tiny islands in the South China Sea is a response to the United States having given Chinese islands in the North China Sea to Japan after the Second World War; China is maneuvering to stop something similar happening again. It is also to be noted that prior to China developing some of these islands in 2014, other islands in the Spratly Islands had been developed by Taiwan, Malaysia, Vietnam and the Philipines for military purposes. China was obviously concerned about being left behind and being unable then to secure its maritime trade routes (Hugar 2016).Hence, from the Chinese standpoint, it is a matter of defense to protect its maritime trade rather than expansion—those tiny islands, actually rocks and reefs, were uninhabited. China is expanding economically on a global scale, but it is doing so peacefully by benefiting a number of countries in its revitalization of the land and maritime Silk Routes. Indeed in China, some have criticized the government for spending vast sums to help other countries when this money should be used internally.

The ultimate vision of modern Chinese Familism is harmony on a worldwide scale. If there was an understanding of Chinese religious values, then there need be no fear of this non-territorial expansion. The trade between the United States and China could instead be mutually beneficial rather than antagonistic. Even the military buildup need not have been seen as a threat. It seems that China would, at an earlier point in time, have preferred a defense pact with the United States. But as the previous US administration promoted Japanese militarism, a threat to China since the late nineteenth century, it instead has been coordinating aspects of its defense with Russia, its traditional enemy, which is still officially at war with Japan. (Because Russia grabbed northern Japanese islands at the end of the Second World War, as well as Chinese territory, a peace treaty between the two has never been signed.)

China is promoted as an enemy and dire threat in the West because it is claimed to be an anti-democracy dictatorship. But this is not how the Chinese understand their government. Different from the West, China has no history of a multiparty electoral system. Based on their history, they understand that without a strong, central authoritarian government, there would be chaos; China has a long history of fragmentation with constant warfare between the fragments. So long as the government continues as a meritocracy with a strong leader subject to the ruling State Council who operates within the concept of Familism as a parent to the Chinese population, the Chinese people are satisfied. They, save students influenced by a naive understanding of the West, feel that they are a truer democracy than that of the West.

Major policies cannot be carried out without the cooperation of the people, even if the policies, after long consultation, are dictated from the top. For example, the one-child policy theoretically went against Familism, but it was embraced by the people, for it was well understood, as I often heard in China before its implementation, *Ren tai duo* ("Too many people"). They knew it was temporary, as it proved to be, and essential for rapid improvement of the economy, as was also the case. It was not so much enforced by the government as it was by local neighborhood and village committees in support of the program.

There has long been an assumption among leaders in the West that capitalism necessarily leads to a representative government, with those who govern chosen by elections. And the West has pushed their model of governance on non-Western countries with missionary fervor and religious zeal. Often this has led to disasters in countries with no history of this type of government, the elections leading to utterly undemocratic repressive governments due to the disappearance of the controls of their previous traditional means of governance connected to traditional indigenous religions.

Examining elected representative governments globally, it seems they are successful where the underlying religion is one of individual salvation, while in countries whose precolonial religion was an aspect of Familism, elections tend to lead to violence and deaths, as in many African nations created by colonial powers ignoring traditional tribal boundaries. Elections work in cultures based on religions of individual salvation, such as Christianity, because it provides the illusion of individual political power. Cultures based on Familism originally tended toward leadership based on clan elders, whose leadership is accepted as paternalistic/maternalistic guidance. For example, among Iroquoian-speaking cultures, which are matrifocal, leaders are chosen from among warriors with oratory skills by a council of Clan Mothers. These male leaders form a subsidiary council subject to the Clan Mother council.

One can interpret Chinese leaders chosen in a similar way by councils within the Chinese Communist Party. With regard to the central government, the large National Party Congress, which meets every five years, chooses a Central Committee, which chooses a Politburo Standing Committee, among whom is chosen the general secretary and the leaders of the various commissions, etc. Similarly, the president, the titular head of the state, is elected by and holds the title at the pleasure of the National People's Congress. Since 1993, both offices have been held by the same person, who is also head of the military commission of the Standing Committee. Hence, although the political leader of China holds considerable power, he is not an autocrat, as claimed by the West, because he holds the offices at the will of large congresses and can be deposed by the same congresses, or even by the presently seven-member Politburo Standing Committee.

As discussed in the previous chapter, Chinese governance was integral with Chinese Religion. The method of choosing those who governed achieved its final form a thousand years ago after a millennium and a half of development. Administrators at various levels (save for the emperor, ideally the hereditary symbolic head of state, as in Britain) were chosen from those who passed a series of examinations based on a fixed body of texts, the Classics, most of which were directly related to Chinese Religion. Advancement among the officials was primarily based on performance reports, although patronage from higher officials also played a role. This mode of government collapsed with the end of imperial rule in the early twentieth century, but it has in essence been revitalized with the Chinese Communist Party, albeit without formal examinations. Hence, Chinese leadership, since the death of Mao (who seems to have suffered from Alzheimer's disease in the last decades of his life), has been by effective leaders who brought new ideas for improving the economy and society, approved by the governing councils. Although plagued with corruption, which has been the bugaboo of Chinese government for a least the last two thousand years (a topic I dealt with regarding the third century in my doctoral dissertation written in the 1960s, see Paper 1987), the Chinese people seem to prefer their tried and tested mode of governance to that of the West.

During the last major student protest, the cry was for "democracy," but the students seemed to have little understanding of the term. When asked by reporters if they wanted elections, they reacted with shock at the suggestion, stating that they wanted to take over the government but did not want elections. In a somewhat similar situation, during the student protest in Hong Kong, students demanded the "democracy" they naively assumed they had under the British. They seemed ignorant of the recent past when Hong Kong was a colony of Britain, governed from London, and policed by South Asians (Sikhs) brought in to control the Chinese population.

When I speak to mature adult Chinese, I receive an entirely different response. For they look with disdain on the type of leaders produced by electoral systems, particularly the last election in the United States. But they also are aware of the situation in Taiwan since the end of martial law. There every time the government reverses with a change in the winning party, school textbooks are rewritten, who is allowed to work in government departments or teach drastically changes, a different large segment of the population loses the right to vote, and one part of the population or the other, depending on how many generations they have been in Taiwan, somewhat represented by the two different parties, feels greatly repressed.

It is worth remembering that Hitler was initially elected to his office of chancellor. H. L. Mencken (1920), a master satirical political critic, has been understood by many to have predicted a century ago the kind of elected leadership the United States has at the present:

> As democracy is perfected, the office represents, more and more closely, the inner soul of the people. We move toward a lofty ideal. On some great and glorious day the plain folks of the land will reach their heart's desire at last, and the White House will be adorned by a downright moron.

Without multiparty elections, which China does not have (it has a one-party system and has, for the last thousand years, chosen its leaders on merit), there is no role for demagogues. Of course, what works for China will not work in the West. In part, this is because the respective histories and the religious foundations are different—they have opposing values regarding the relationship between the individual and society.

Conclusion

It is this difference in religious foundations which lies at the heart of the US desire to destroy present-day China. A think piece produced by the Strategic Services Institute of the US War College in part concludes:

> The United States and China have been at odds ever since the founding of the PRC in 1949. . . . To the United States, China's rise and its external impact are very worrisome. Among many other factors, the fact that this rising China is in the hands of an authoritarian government, whose leaders do not share with their American counterparts on the fundamental values under-pinning the U.S.-led international order, is very troublesome to the United States. (Lai 2011: 96–7)

Thus, the American missionary zeal to Christianize China continues, along with the US government's zeal to covert China to its version of democracy. To this end, it not only engages in false propaganda regarding freedom of religion, but it, along with tyrannical regimes in the Central Asian part of the former Soviet Union, supports Uighur independence, including terrorism, created and maintains a Tibetan government-in-exile in India, and continues to arm Taiwan. As I write this in 2019, the United States is engaged in an economic war with China for the purpose of inhibiting China's advancing to technological superiority. The same US strategic think piece predicts that as China gains military parity with the United States, it would take but a spark to ignite an all-out war. It is frightening to realize that the clash between Western Christian missionaries and Familism in China that began in the mid-nineteenth century could end in a global conflagration.

Why Buddhism Succeeded and Christianity Failed in China

Introduction

Some foreign religious traditions became transformed in the Chinese cultural milieu to the point of becoming an element of Chinese Religion itself, such as Buddhism. By adapting aspects of normative Chinese Religion, some comfortably fit into the Chinese religious gestalt as minority traditions, such as Islam and Judaism. Others rigidly rejected accommodation to the Chinese worldview and morality and at times were expelled by the Chinese government, such as Christianity.

The histories of the three interconnected Abrahamic traditions in China are quite different from that of Buddhism and from each other. Judaism and Islam did not proselytize in China and adapted to Chinese life and culture without in turn influencing it. In doing so, they became part of the Chinese cultural matrix and survived for a considerable period of time. Muslims were present in much larger numbers and, given that some countries in Central Asia contiguous with China converted to Islam, never lost contact with the Islamic world. They remain a large viable presence in China today. After a half-millennium, Judaism in China lost contact with Judaism elsewhere. This combined with its relatively small numbers led to its slow decline, albeit the Kaifeng synagogue was viable as long as the European synagogue with the longest history there.

The Christian experience is quite dissimilar. Save for Nestorian Christian merchants present in China during the Tang period, aside from merchants, Christians came to China as missionaries and sought to convert China to Christianity and a European way of life. The missionaries were supported by European powers that used them as a tool in their failed attempt to colonize China as they had India, the Philippines, Southeast Asia, and Indonesia. The anti-Chinese attitudes and destructive behavior toward Chinese notions of good order by first the Vatican and later by Protestant missionaries led to Christian missionaries and converts being hated by many Chinese and, at various times, expelled or massacred.

The Buddhist experience in China

Buddhist merchants entered China with the inception of the Silk Road in the early Han period. By this time, several cultures along the Silk Road in southern Central Asia had become Buddhist, so their presence was noticed by the Chinese. A monastery to serve these numerous Buddhist merchants was built in the then capital of Loyang.

The collapse of the Han dynasty in the early third century was as disruptive to the Chinese world as was the collapse of the western part of the Roman Empire to the Romans. The Chinese empire became fragmented into several kingdoms and within a century descended into political chaos and economic collapse. The Chinese lost faith in the ability of traditional ideologies to solve their problems and became open to new ideas.

The expanding growth of Buddhist monasteries at this time necessitated altering the standard rules of Buddhist monasticism, which forbade monks to handle weapons or money. To survive raids by brigands during this period of disorder, the monasteries were walled and monks began to be trained in martial arts. Given the practice of lay members contributing to the monasteries to gain merit toward salvation, they also became repositories for wealth. This wealth led to the monasteries becoming proto-banks, as money could be lent to those in need at interest. The monasteries became the means for social order for the peasantry, and Buddhism, the first proselytizing religion, rapidly spread among the Chinese.

When the north was invaded, China became fractured into two halves. The non-Chinese rulers in the northern part of China capitalized on this new adherence by co-opting the religion, with the ruler taking on the role of head of a state-sponsored Buddhist church, much as the English monarch is the head of the Anglican Church. The various Buddhist sects from India that were present in China, never fully understood by the Chinese, were becoming increasingly Sinicized. In the south, the gentry became supporters of these newly Sinicized Buddhist sects, as well as the developing Daoist churches.

By the seventh century, at the inception of the second major successful Chinese empire, the Tang, Chinese Buddhism had become dominant within the broader context of Chinese Familism. Daoism had developed into several institutional religions on the model of the Buddhist sects and vied for supremacy with Buddhism. The two traditions competed for imperial support, as did the various Buddhist sects with each other.

At times, the wealth and power of Buddhist institutions rivaled or surpassed that of the state and were seen as a challenge to governmental authority. The state then cracked down on the institutional aspects to weaken the monasteries but was never concerned about the beliefs and religious practices of individuals. No attempt was made to end Buddhism, but the government acted to ensure its own continued existence by weakening a rival institution.

In the mid-eighth century, the chief general of the military staged a coup d'état against the Tang dynasty. The court fled and seeking financial resources to resist the insurgency expanded the sale of certificates of ordination. Many thousands purchased these certificates since Buddhist monks were released from the obligation of paying taxes for the rest of their lives, while there was no requirement that they actually live as a monk. This had the immediate effect of raising funds to put down the revolt, but China ended up as a nation with a huge number of non-tax paying monks and monasteries. This increased the tax burden on the remaining part of the population and reached the point where it was cheaper for whole villages to nominally become monks and nuns, donate their farmland to monasteries, and then rent them back for less than the land tax.

With the government finally teetering on financial ruin in the mid-ninth century, it again cracked down on the monasteries. Regulations were promulgated that limited the number of monasteries in a district, the amount of land a monastery could own, the number of monks and nuns resident in a monastery, and the number and size of its bronze images (the melting of bronze coins to cast images created a monetary crisis—see Gernet 1956). This was suppression of institutions rather than persecution of beliefs and ritual practices. Lay Buddhists seem to have been unaffected. A Japanese monk traveled extensively throughout China at this time and made no mention of the suppression in his diary (Reischauer 1955); obviously, it had not affected him.

After the removal of the economic basis of Buddhist institutions, only those sects that had become fully Sinicized continued. These include Chan (Japanese: Zen), which appealed to the literati as it was complementary to the *Zhuangzi* in many respects; *Tiantai*, which amalgamated and harmonized the various Buddhist ideologies and thus appealed to intellectuals; and the major one, the Pure Land sect, which had radically changed to focus on assisting Chinese Religion.

Pure Land Buddhism originally offered a pleasant realm upon death attained through faith in the saving power of Amida Buddha to support meditation to achieve Nirvana. The concept of the Pure Land or Western Paradise changed to a permanent heaven, offering a pleasant abode for the family dead. Buddhist monks were hired to chant masses for the family's deceased, and name plaques were added to monasteries so the dead could benefit from the chanting of sutras. For the last thousand years, Buddhism has mainly been an integral albeit optional part of Chinese Religion supporting Familism and its essential theology by adding aspects not present before the integration of Buddhism.

During the preceding centuries, with the reestablishment of a unified China, a homogeneous culture, and pride in it, Buddhism was increasingly being viewed as an alien religion. Buddhism became perceived as un-Chinese for many reasons, especially with regard to Familism. At that time, becoming a monk or nun meant denying family ties, and by being chaste, monks and nuns do not continue the family line. This, for a religion, society, and culture that focused on family and filial piety, was anathema. Besides, Chinese did not consider chastity a healthy practice and assumed that the monks and nuns—who shared the same monasteries—were illicitly having sex. Given that many of these monks and nuns were only so for reasons of taxation, there may have been some truth to many of the folktales about the licentiousness of monks (similar to those in England at the time of Chaucer).

The combination of removing the economic basis of the monasteries, thus ending their power, combined with increasing anti-Buddhist feelings, led to the demise of Buddhism in China as a powerful force and a dominant aspect of religion. Only those forms that had become fully Sinicized survived, and Buddhism continued as a minor aspect of Chinese Religion. Not until the twentieth century did Buddhism again become popular among Chinese as an institutional alternative to Christianity, which was detested by the majority of Chinese for the reasons that will become clear in the second part of this chapter.

Not only had major aspects of Buddhism become integrated into normative Chinese Religion, but Chinese Religion had become partially transformed by Buddhism, particularly with regard to concepts of life after death, although these were far removed from the original Buddhist concepts from India.

Buddhism along with Daoism also came to function as adjuncts to normative Chinese Religion. They became similar to the role of the mystery cults in relation to the family and civic rites of Hellenistic and Roman culture, or Masonry with regard to Christianity and Judaism in modern Western culture. They offered not only intercession and support for the family dead but also means for individual transformation. Buddhism offered various forms of meditation with the goal of enlightenment, and Daoism theoretically offered techniques not only for prolonging life but for becoming a *xian*, a fully realized person in body and in mind. The concept of the Bodhisattva led to a transformation of Chinese deities, who by the Song period were ghosts of particular deceased human beings who could shower divine beneficence on living humans. The Buddhist concept of Nirvana was transformed into one of salvation into a pleasant realm of the dead modeled on life on earth, a Sino-Buddhist heaven. The integration of these institutional adjuncts into noninstitutional Chinese Religion, saw, for example, the previously mentioned customs of bringing in Daoist priests to officiate at funerals and Buddhist monks or nuns to chant masses for the dead.

Buddhism also offered services in China not hitherto present there. Since monasteries were often built in scenic places, especially picturesque mountains, they offered hostels for both pilgrims and tourists. At Shitou Shan (Lionhead Mountain) in central Taiwan, for example, small monasteries along the scenic ridge trail offer lodgings for the night and vegetarian meals.

Monasteries also provided safe haven for retired political and military leaders. Controversial government ministers and failed generals could often retire as a monk and avoid possible repercussions due to their careers. Women who did not wish to marry and subject themselves to their husband's family, especially their mother-in-law who would control her life, could become nuns. Similarly,

Figure 22 A monastery atop Shitou Shan (Lion's Head Mountain) in central Taiwan (ca. 1965). The center building is the worship hall which backs into a natural cave. On one side of the courtyard are dormitory style rooms for monks and male tourists and on the other side are the same for nuns and female tourists.

a woman whose husband died and had no son to support her might choose to become a nun. Becoming a Buddhist monk or nun did not have the expectation that a Catholic monastic life might have, since vows were not permanent. All that was expected was to lead a simple life and perform a modicum of work in the monastery, including the chanting of masses. If one had financial resources, then a donation to the monastery meant there would be no expectations of labor. It would be a home in which, if one fell ill, one would receive care for the rest of one's life.

In present-day Hong Kong and Taiwan, Buddhism is surging in popular appeal. Buddhism is perceived as an acceptable alternative to Christianity, especially since it has proven capable of providing modern religious institutional amenities. Today, there are Buddhist universities, hospitals, and charitable organizations. Two sects in Taiwan, Tzu Chi and Fo Guang Shan, have achieved enormous growth and large physical headquarters, and, reflecting the past, support different political parties. They both have active branches in North America.

The Christian experience in China

It is not until the Tang period that we have evidence for Christianity in China. A stele (inscribed stone monument) dated to 781 was erected by a Syrian Nestorian Christian to commemorate the building of a monastery for twenty-one monks in the capital by order of the imperial government. (It was common for the government as a courtesy to build monasteries—given the Buddhist model— for communities of foreign merchants.) There is no indication of proselytizing, suggesting that these priests were serving a community of foreign Christians. Thus, Nestorian Christian merchants resided in the foreign community along with Muslims, Manichaeans, and possibly Jews. Following the collapse of the Tang dynasty, there is no further indication of a Nestorian presence in China.

A few of the Christian clergy made it to the Mongol capital (in the thirteenth and fourteenth centuries), but the Polo family are the first Christians that we know of to have reached China itself at that time. Even fewer Christian missionaries went beyond Mongolia to China. The last we can be certain of is the papal legate, John of Marignolli, who arrived in 1342 and stayed for several years.

For the next two centuries, there is no record of a Christian presence until missionaries attempted to enter China when the Portuguese arrived in the second half of the sixteenth century. This begins one of the most bizarre chapters in Christian history, as well as Chinese religious history. It is a chapter that has yet to end, as it continues to inform US foreign policy and attitudes toward

China today. The history of Christianity in China is essentially one of European and later American colonial imperialism which clashed with China's sense of its own sovereignty and destiny.

A Papal Bull of 1493, followed by a treaty a year later, split the world outside of Europe between Spain and Portugal. Of course, the Papal Bull was not recognized by Protestant countries, or, for that matter, by the established civilizations in Asia. It was based on an understanding that Spain would colonize westward into the "New World," also known as "New Spain." Portugal would colonize eastward, going around the Cape of Good Hope to India and China. But the dividing line put most of Brazil in the hands of Portugal, and Spain, by going around the tip of South America, could establish a foothold in East Asia by attaching the Philippines to New Spain. Thus the Spanish could bring Chinese goods across the Pacific to Acapulco, where the yearly galleon was offloaded and the goods transported overland to Veracruz, from where they would be shipped across the Atlantic to Spain. Jesuit missionaries, whether German, Italian, or French, thus necessarily worked either with the Portuguese or the Spanish fleets and military.

Portugal attained from the Chinese government the right to trade through Macau in 1535 and began a settlement which became permanent in 1557. The Spanish reached the Philippines in 1521 with their Portuguese admiral, Magellan, and began their first settlement in 1565. There they massacred tens of thousands of Chinese merchants in 1603, considering them to be unwanted competition. Foreign trade in the late fifteenth and early sixteenth century, for both Portugal and Spain, was simple brigandage. A town would be attacked, its inhabitants massacred, and its valuables stolen. The Chinese at first considered, quite rightfully, the Europeans to be no different than the Japanese pirates wreaking havoc on the Chinese coast, which had led the Chinese court to attempt to halt Chinese from trading abroad and foreigners from entering China by sea.

From the beginning of the Portuguese settlement in Macau, Jesuit missionaries sought permission to penetrate into China. While in Macau, they studied Chinese language and culture. In 1583, two Jesuits received permission to live in a town near Guangdong (Canton) close to Macau. To fit in, being monks themselves, at first they wore the garb of Buddhist monks. They soon learned that Buddhist monks were then held in disrepute and sought to blend in among the elite by becoming literati. They studied the Classics, learned the language of government officials—different from the local languages—and took on the garb, illicitly at first, of the literati. In 1601, one of these two, Matteo Ricci, received permission to reside in the capital of Beijing. Soon he was joined by other Jesuits.

Given their study of the Chinese Classics, along with their knowledge of European science and technology, the Jesuits were accepted as scholars and provided with the usual government support. Eventually, some received official titles and offices. Ricci admired the teachings found in the Classics and understood China to be at a stage of development just prior to Christianity that would be receptive to the Christian message. He promulgated this understanding in *Relations* (letters) sent to Europe, in which he deliberately misleadingly described Chinese Religion as triune—"Three Chinese Religions," as discussed in Chapter 2.

Ricci was successful in "converting"—in the Jesuit mode which added Christian rituals to family, clan, and state rituals—two members of the prestigious Hanlin Academy and an imperial prince. Slowly others among the elite also became Christians. Twice in the early part of the seventeenth century the Jesuit mission was nearly terminated due to a suspicion of sedition, but the support they received from powerful members of the government saved them.

When fighting began to take place between the invading Manchu armies and the Ming dynasty, the Jesuits hedged their bets by supporting both sides. That support included the casting of European style cannons. Thus, when the Manchus took control of China and instituted a new dynasty, Jesuits were highly regarded by the first Manchu emperors. They were given charge of the bureau of astronomy and the calendar, and were also charged with mapping China; one was a court painter. They continued to manufacture cannons, and the Jesuit mission increased in size and influence within the court.

By the end of the seventeenth century, Franciscan and Dominican missionaries were arriving in China. Different from the Jesuits, they proselytized among the general population. The number of conversions was counted by the missionaries to be in the hundreds of thousands. Not only were these figures undoubtedly inflated, but most of these numbers reflect *in articulo mortis*, the practice of baptizing dead infants. It has also to be taken into account that the Jesuits controlled employment in a major government ministry.

From the mid-seventeenth century, the Christian missions suffered a series of setbacks. The first and most important of these was the Rites Controversy. Franciscans and Dominicans considered the Jesuit mode of Christian conversion heretical; from their perspective, the Jesuits were allowing Christian converts to continue heathenish practices. The Jesuits understood that if the family rites were forbidden for Chinese Christians, they would no longer be Chinese. And if the state rites were forbidden for Chinese Christians, they could not be among the elite. The Vatican vacillated for well over a century, from 1628 to 1742, but increasingly went against the Jesuit position. Ironically, the Second Vatican Council in the early 1960s reversed that position and allowed Chinese Catholics to reverence their ancestors. Family shrines with daily offerings of incense are again to be found in Chinese Catholic homes.

The Jesuits had asked the Kangxi emperor, at the time the most powerful political figure in the world, the Manchu Empire then at its largest and strongest, for his viewpoint. Of course, he decided in favor of the Jesuit position. When the Vatican came down against that position, it meant that a foreign power was not only contradicting him but ordering religious practices for the Chinese in China. Kangxi gave the missionaries the choice of obeying him or leaving China. The results of this insult to Chinese sovereignty remains today. Only a Catholic Church not beholden to the Vatican is allowed to function in China. No religious organization that is actually controlled by a foreign authority is legitimate there.

The second major setback was the abolition of the Society of Jesus in 1773. Some Jesuits elected to remain in China as secular priests. Although there were several expulsions of missionaries, those that held government offices were allowed to stay. In 1805, there was a suspicion that missionaries were planning an invasion by Europeans, and the edicts against Christianity were more rigorously enforced. From then until the Opium Wars in the mid-nineteenth century, Christianity could only continue underground in China. In any case, after the Vatican dictated that Chinese Christians must, in effect, stop being ethnically Chinese, Christianity held little appeal for most Chinese.

The next chapter in the history of Christianity in China will be very briefly summarized. These developments in the Christian presence in China still continue and are the essential background to understanding contemporary China, Christianity in China, and the twentieth-century wars involving the West with China and contiguous countries. (For a compact yet detailed history of Christianity in China, especially for the last century, with analyses from a Christian perspective, see Bays 2012.)

By the beginning of the nineteenth century, China was suffering from the familiar pattern of dynastic decline: weak emperors brought up by eunuchs inside the palace who were ignorant about the world around them, an increasingly corrupt officialdom, peasant land falling into the hands of distant landowners and peasants thereby becoming impoverished, and a poorly equipped and trained military due to corruption and a weak central government. This usual pattern was exacerbated by the increasing difficulty of maintaining the far-flung empire the Manchu attached to China proper when it conquered the Ming dynasty. Simultaneously, Europe was gaining military might through advances in weapons technology, originally from China, and an increased taste for colonial expansion brought about by the Industrial Revolution and the resultant search for raw materials and markets for its manufactured goods.

Britain, in particular, as did the Roman world two thousand years before, was suffering from an imbalance of trade with China: they imported tea, silk, and pottery ("china"), but they had nothing which the Chinese wished to purchase. Britain sought to solve this economic problem through a triangular trade. The British East Indies company sold manufactured goods, particular cotton cloth, to its colony of India, where the ships picked up opium, grown in Afghanistan. The opium was sold in China, where the ships picked up tea and other luxury goods to be transported back to Britain. The British pursued this strategy in contravention of Chinese laws that prohibited the importation of opium. China had sufficient opium grown internally for traditional medicinal purposes.

When a British ship brought a load of opium to the extreme south of China in 1839, a strong provincial governor confiscated the shipload and burned it, prompting Britain to declare war on China. After losing the initial sea battle, the by-now inept imperial government at the far north of China, which had little interest in the distant south, considered the British navy a minor nuisance not worth the expenditure of building a proper navy, and sued for peace in 1842.

The treaty following the "First Opium War" saw Hong Kong ceded to the British—to the Chinese government, it was a distant, tiny and inconsequential island—and the opening of five ports to foreign trade on the mainland. Foreigners were given extraterritoriality, but they were to remain in the treaty ports. A most-favored-nation clause meant that whatever one Western nation obtained through treaty applied to all other Western nations. Religion was left ambiguous in the treaty, but missionaries began to enter the treaty ports. Most importantly, the West learned that the weak Chinese government would not defend itself, the flood of manufactured Western goods eroded the Chinese economy, and cheap opium in a time of increasing socioeconomic despair debilitated Chinese society.

The European countries soon sought to increase their gains and looked for an excuse for another war. In 1856, a small Chinese ship with a crew of twelve was caught smuggling and the crew arrested by the Chinese government. The British claimed the ship was from Hong Kong and therefore exempt from Chinese import regulations, and demanded the release of the Chinese crew. At the same time, a French Catholic priest caught in the midst of civil strife was killed in the interior. These were the excuses Britain and France sought, and they declared war on China. The Chinese were caught up in suppressing the Taiping rebellion and again sued for peace in 1860, thus ending the "Second Opium War," which was actually a continuation of the first.

The treaty that followed was disastrous for China. More ports were opened to foreign trade as well as the entire Yangtze River, and foreigners could travel anywhere in China with full extraterritoriality. Massive indemnities were claimed which bankrupted China and were used to support missionaries. The treaty made specific provision for the toleration of Christianity. Most importantly, all Chinese who converted to Christianity were provided with extraterritoriality, which meant that any Chinese who became a Christian was no longer subject to Chinese civil or criminal law. The French-language version of the treaty had one further stipulation not in the Chinese version: French missionaries could seize land and erect buildings anywhere with the protection of the French army.

The treaty resulted in a massive influx of missionaries, who protected their converts under any and all circumstances, including the commission of crimes. During famines, children were bought by the missions, and food was offered only to those who converted. Missionaries could take any land they wanted to build churches. A Christian convert could claim his neighbor's land as Christian converts automatically won civil cases. "The chief problems . . . were the arrogation of official status to themselves by some missionaries and their interference in local government, and the refusal of Chinese converts to abide by the laws of China" (Bays 2012: 76). These and other outrages led to increasing massive hatred of missionaries and Chinese converts among the general population (see Latourette 1929: 276–77 and 280).

At the same time, an indigenous Chinese Christian development, the Taiping Movement, snowballed into a revolt against the detested foreign Manchu (Qing) dynasty. Unlike the partially assimilated Islam and Judaism, the movement was based on a fully-fledged Chinese reinterpretation of the Bible and the Christian message.

The Taiping Movement's roots lay in a vision an educated Chinese had in a fever delirium that years later led him to believe he was the younger brother of Christ. This was attested to by mediums who became possessed by the Holy Spirit and by God. Western monotheism was understood according to the Chinese polytheism and the family model: the Trinity was understood as three separate deities, and a married Christ was perceived as part of a large holy family. This was a Christianity that made sense to a large number of Chinese, and the religio-political military movement that arose from it was quite successful, conquering much of central China.

The leaders of the Taiping Movement instituted a new regime, with this younger brother of Christ and his wife as the emperor and consort, and their capital in Nanjing as the New Jerusalem. A Chinese translation of the Bible replaced the Classics as the basis of the civil service examinations. They also took from the West religious intolerance and destroyed other religious establishments. (For a more detailed discussion and analysis of the Taiping Movement, see Paper 1995b: Chapter 9.)

To the European Christian missionaries, a Chinese messiah was anathema, and for the European governments, a new strong Chinese government was undesirable. Thus they combined their armies with the Chinese army, under the command of a British general, to put down the Taiping Movement. By1861, much of China was thoroughly devastated and many millions had died, adding further hatred of Christianity and European imperialism. The Manchu government was rendered virtually defunct.

Following a war with Japan that China lost in 1895 and the loss of far northern China to Russia at the same time, an attempt at reform in 1898 resulted in foreigners gaining even more control of China, such as Roman Catholic missionaries having complete sovereignty over their parishes. Severe flooding and a series of poor harvests along with the Chinese hatred of foreign missionaries and their Chinese converts boiled over into the officially sanctioned "Boxer Rebellion" of 1900. The bottled-up rage exploded throughout China and many missionaries and converts were killed. The foreign legations were besieged in their compounds in Beijing until rescued by Western armies. The result was a reign of terror by foreign armies, the murder of large numbers of non-Christian Chinese (emperor of Germany: "No quarter will be given, no prisoners will be taken"). Many of the surviving missionaries and Chinese Christians joined in the general mayhem and looting.

By the beginning of the twentieth century, the Chinese government was in effect taken over by foreigners and China was broken up into European quasi-colonies. The United States, through its "Open Door Policy," claimed all rights and privileges won by Europeans everywhere in China. The American people came to perceive China as theirs through the expanding number of American missionaries, and American Navy ships patrolled the Yangtze River to protect missionaries and their converts.

Western powers controlled Chinese taxation and used the money to support missionary activities. Some of this money was put toward education. The only means to a modern Western education was through Christian missions, schools, and universities, and almost all of the modern educated Chinese elite in the first half of the twentieth century received their education, both in China and the West, via Christianity. Thus, a number of the educated became Protestants.

Within a decade, the Manchu dynasty collapsed, and China fragmented into regional warlord rule. A nationalist movement was begun under Chinese Christian political theorists and generals, but initial success led to rampant corruption and the breakaway of a competing communist movement. Sun Zhongshan (Sun Yat-sen), the founder of the Republic of China and its first president, was highly influenced by Protestantism, and Jiang Zhoutai (Chiang Kai-shek), the head of the Nationalist Army and later president in Taiwan, and his wife were nominally Methodists. Thus the Nationalist Party was perceived as Christian and the Chinese Communist Party as atheist by the United States. The United States understood the civil war in China to be a religious one, a war between Christians and "Godless" communists.

The aftermath of the Japanese invasion and the Second World War was a civil war won by the Communist Party by defeating the Nationalist Party, which was by that time thoroughly corrupt. One of the first acts of the new government was to rid China of the hated foreign missionaries, with the exception of particular individuals, predominantly those from Canada, who had played no role in imperialism and had not gained the enmity of the people.

The strongest central government China had seen in a century and a half offered the hand of friendship to the United States, but under the influence of Senator Knowland and the "China Lobby," the United States viewed the government as godless usurpers of the rightful Christian government allied with the United States, whose remnants they protected and supported in Taiwan. These attitudes, to a degree, still influence American policy and continued covert activity against China, as previously discussed.

From long experience in the United States, I have noticed that many Americans express a visceral hatred of China and Chinese, because they cannot forgive China for not becoming American-controlled Christians.

> For more than a century, Americans have had special, even romantic notions about China becoming a "Christian nation," one modeling itself after the US. . . . . When China fell under CCP control in 1949, there arose American disappointment and anger at how China had been, as it were, hijacked from friendship with the US and the blessings of Christianity. (Bays 2012: 203)

This perceived American failure in China can be interpreted as a thwarted God-given Manifest Destiny of a constant push westward, from the Atlantic colonies to taking over the indigenous farms and towns in the Midwest, to the "Indian Wars" on the Plains, and across the Pacific to the colonization of Hawaii, the Philippines and finally China (see Drinnon 1980). Such frustration has led to wars.

Being theoretically Marxist, the Chinese Communist Party expressed a negative attitude toward religion in general, and adopted the Christian missionary attitude toward nominal Chinese Religion as mindless superstition, not worthy of the term "religion." This attitude reached its peak in the gross excesses of the Cultural Revolution (1966-76), which saw the destruction of religious buildings, as well as many old structures in general, regardless of religious orientation. A few years after the end of the Cultural Revolution, observing an elderly woman making offerings at a Buddhist shrine, I asked her what religion she was practicing. She responded that she was practicing *mixin* (superstition)—she was not being sarcastic but actually thought that was the proper term for her religion.

The collapse of the Cultural Revolution, with its enmity toward traditional Chinese culture and a decade-long educational hiatus, saw people flood the few reopened Christian churches, expecting to learn about Western science and technology, given the earlier linkage of Christian missions to an education in Western science. The rejoicing of American Christians over this massive turnout soon was lost as people quickly turned away when they received Christian sermons rather than lectures on nuclear physics or computer technology. Presently, a number of Christian sects are legitimate religions in China but none are under foreign control. The number of Christians in China often claimed by American church statistics tends to be grossly inflated.

The Chinese government for decades allowed an indigenous Catholic Church but not one subject to the Vatican. Hence, the effect of the Vatican decision in the Rites Controversy nearly three centuries ago continued to reverberate in China. Thus, there was a licit Catholic Church registered with the government and an underground illicit Catholic Church connected to the Vatican. But in September 2018 this split situation began to come to an end:

> The Vatican and China said yesterday they had signed a historic agreement on the appointment of Roman Catholic bishops, a breakthrough on an issue that for decades fueled tensions between the Holy See and Beijing and thwarted efforts toward diplomatic relations. . . . The Vatican said that, as part of the deal, the pope would recognize seven Chinese bishops who were appointed by Beijing without the Vatican's approval, and were excommunicated as illegitimate. Sources told Reuters the accord gave the Vatican a say in the naming of bishops and granted the pope veto power over candidates. China's Catholics are split

between an underground church swearing loyalty to the Vatican, and the state-supervised Catholic Patriotic Association (CPA). (theguardian.com/world/20 18/sep/22/vatican-pope-francis-agreement-with-china-nominating-bishops)

Various surveys over the last two decades tend to find that slightly more than 2 percent of the population of China identify themselves as Christian, the majority being Protestant. The Catholic Church in China is split between the licit and illicit modes, the latter primarily in the countryside. It can be expected that somehow the split will end following the agreement between the Vatican and the Chinese government. The licit Protestant Church tends to be found in the larger cities. The illicit "house churches," predominantly Pentecostal, are primarily found in towns, and a reliable estimate of their numbers is unavailable, given that members of an illicit organization are less likely to self-identify. The huge numbers given by various American organizations tend to be understood as fantasy by scholars.

Elsewhere in East Asia, the Korean and Vietnam wars were fought by the United States in part because of a perceived threat posed by "godless" communism to Christian regimes. In Vietnam, Buddhist monks supported the communist regime, because the government of the south was attempting to force Catholicism over the indigenous Vietnamese religion that combined Familism and Buddhism. In Taiwan, the party promoting independence from China is strongly supported by American evangelical Protestant sects—the Taiwan Presbyterian Church and the Democratic Progressive Party seeking independence are virtually one. (The Nationalist Party, when it was the sole legal party due to martial law, was led by Methodists and considered itself the government of all of China.) Everywhere in East Asia, Christianity and politics have always been inseparable.

Conclusion

Thus, the history of Christianity in China is vastly different from the history of Islam and Judaism in China, both of which successfully assimilated to become a part of the Chinese cultural fabric. For the latter two religions, there was neither proselytizing nor missionaries functioning as an advance for colonial imperialism. Chinese Muslims and Jews maintained their Chinese ethnic identity alongside their religious Muslim and Jewish identities. Chinese Jews were fully accepted in China for they had neither the inclination nor the ability to raise the ire of the Chinese. A number became civil and military officials, as did

Chinese Muslims, and the Jews in Kaifeng, with the support of the government, built a magnificent synagogue complex that may have been the largest ever built anywhere. (There were six larger synagogue communities in the seaports, but we have no information regarding them.)

Christianity, particularly Protestantism, did grow in China in the early twentieth century, especially given that a Western education was virtually only obtainable through Christian institutions both in China and abroad. But Christianity did not become part of the Chinese religious fabric, as did Buddhism, because, as recognized by Kenneth Scott Latourette, the foremost scholar of the Christian missions in China and a missionary himself, the theological understandings are incompatible, and Chinese theology imbued every aspect of Chinese culture and society: "Since Christianity necessarily runs counter to so much that is an integral part of Chinese culture . . . It can succeed only by bringing enough force to bear and for a sufficient period to work a revolution" (1929: 44). If one considers communism a Protestant heresy, as some Church historians have, then Latourette can be seen as a prophet as communism did succeed in China through revolution. But the Chinese Communist Party, subtly influenced by Chinese Religion, fought against Christian destruction of Chinese culture—both Western Christian missionizing and, to a lesser degree, the Christian influenced Nationalist Party—and continues to do so today.

Bays notes that "most who considered the matter concluded that . . . Christianity had been a failed venture in China," although he disagrees, as he continues, "Of course, reality has been different" (Bays 2012: 203). Bays is potentially correct. In comparing the Buddhist and Christian experiences in China, of considerable importance is time. It took eight centuries for Buddhism to become fully integrated into the Chinese religious complex, both influencing normative practices of Chinese Religion and the "Confucianism" of the literati elite. During that time, Buddhism became radically transformed from its South Asian origins. It is this Sinicized Buddhism that went on to flourish in Korea, Japan, and Vietnam. Christianity has only been present in China (excluding the earlier period of Jesuit, Franciscan and Dominican missionizing) for less than two centuries, much of that time wedded to Western colonialism. As Christianity is now beginning to develop indigenously (see Bays 2012: 193–99), and if it changes to complement the theology of Chinese Religion, as Buddhism did, then over time it too might be as successful.

The Theology of the Chinese Jews: A Synthesis of Judaism and Neo-Confucianism

Introduction: The Kaifeng Jewish community

Around a thousand years ago, Jewish merchants, originally from Persia (which then would have included modern Iraq) and residing in one of the six Chinese seaport Jewish communities, were invited by the government, perhaps regarding the importation of cotton from India, to settle in the then capital of Kaifeng. By a century later, with government support, they built a synagogue based on Chinese architecture. Twice rebuilt following floods, it became one of the largest in the world, when the various auxiliary buildings on a plot of land as large as a football pitch are included.

Over the centuries, the Kaifeng Jews assimilated to Chinese culture, while maintaining a traditional Jewish life (see Simons 2010), with some becoming learned in the Chinese Classics, as well as Torah (first five books of the Hebrew Bible). Through the seaport synagogues, they remained in contact with Judaism in Baghdad and elsewhere. The assimilation followed the normal Judaic pattern when expanding to new areas. For example, Ashkenazi Jews originally moved from Germany to Eastern Europe around the same time. Their language became Yiddish, a Germanic language with Turkish elements, their appearance became generally Slavic, and their clothes, cuisine, and so forth reflects premodern northeastern European and Baltic preferences. Over time, the Chinese Jews similarly shifted their daily language from Judeo-Persian to Chinese (reserving Hebrew for ritual use), adopted Chinese cuisine while keeping kosher, and added to the traditional practices more elaborate memorializing of the dead of the family with relevant practices from Chinese Religion (see Paper 2012a).

By the seventeenth century, members of the Kaifeng synagogue community passed the highest of the civil service examinations and achieved important government positions. (How the Chinese Jews maintained a normative Jewish life while functioning as magistrates, given their priestly role analyzed in Chapter 6, is extensively discussed in Paper 2017.) At that time, they came into contact with Jesuit missionaries, who recorded their religious practices and understandings, the design and furnishings of the synagogue, the inscriptions in Chinese on large stelae, and the calligraphy on the many Chinese-style placards which decorated the synagogue in both Hebrew and Chinese. It is this data that provides us with information about the community and an entrée into their theological understanding. All of this material, both in Chinese and English translation (retranslated in Paper 2012), will be found in White 1966.

A half-century earlier, the government, after a period of massive, costly maritime expeditions, ended sea trade and, in response to pirate attacks, moved the population away from the coastal areas. This brought to an end the port synagogue communities and the Kaifeng community's means for contact with Judaism elsewhere. In the early nineteenth century, the Yellow River, "China's Sorrow," again flooded, destroying Kaifeng and the synagogue. In the mid-nineteenth century, after the death of the last rabbi, a massive civil insurrection against the foreign Manchu dynasty, the Taiping Movement (discussed in the

Figure 23 Although the Kaifeng synagogue no longer exists, one can see what the synagogue looked like by visiting the Grand Mosque in Xi'an, which was built around the same time with the same architecture, and the grounds and buildings were of the same size and layout. This is the main hall of the mosque, and the exterior of the main hall of the Kaifeng synagogue probably would have looked the same (the interiors of course would be different).

preceding chapter), ravaged Kaifeng and dispersed the population. The Judaism of the Kaifeng Jews had come to a functional end, but the Kaifeng synagogue community had lasted as long as the oldest continuously functioning synagogue in Europe. Remnants of this community returned and their descendants still live in Kaifeng. (For a history of the Kaifeng Jews, see Leslie 1972).

Background I: The Literati understanding of essential reality

For well over the last thousand years, with roots going back another fifteen hundred years, elite status in China derived from passing a series of examinations based on a small, fixed body of texts, the "Classics." Passing the civil service examinations made one eligible for appointment to high government offices, the only path to both wealth and prestige. Those who passed the first of these examinations were officially recognized as being in a class above ordinary people.

All intellectual and later artistic endeavors arose from this sociopolitical class: the scholar-officials or literati. Since the inception of the first successful Chinese empire 2,200 years ago, literati ideology, the ideology of government officials, was in a constant process of synthesis, bringing together most of the diverse streams of Chinese thought. This ever-evolving ideology is called *rujia* (commonly mistranslated as "Confucianism"). Two thousand years ago, the various schools of thought were synthesized; thus, five phases and yin-yang theory, as well as the basic texts of Daojia, were combined with the thought of Kongzi, Xunzi, and Mengzi. A thousand years or so ago, Daojiao and aspects of Buddhist thought, especially that of Chan, were amalgamated into a synthesis called Neo-Confucianism in the West.

Chinese thought in comparison with the thought found in Indo-European language speaking cultures is highly pragmatic; abstractions are avoided, not being readily expressed in the language. For example, in literary Chinese one can write of something being beautiful or of a statement being true, but there is no way to express "truth" or "beauty" in the abstract. In part, this is due to the nature of written Chinese which remained logographic and which contemporary neurological research has shown to lead to different parts of the brain being used in thinking than in traditions with alphabetic or syllabic writing systems (see Chapter 2).

Hence, although a school of logic developed in China at the same time it was developing in Greece, it was eventually deemed useless, since formal logic is more theoretical than practical. Similarly, formal grammar never developed in premodern China, as it is based on the concept of formal logic.

The extant early text on logic, the *Kongsun longzi*, dating to about 2,500 years ago, has two famous statements that are explicated in terms of logic. One is "White horse is not horse," seemingly meaning the nonsensical statement, "A white horse is not a horse," but actually a statement of set theory: {white horse} ≠ {horse}. The second is "There is nothing that cannot be pointed to [literally: 'fingered'] and yet that which is pointed to is not the pointing [lit.: a finger is not a finger]."

The earliest text of Daoist thought, the early strata of the *Zuangzi* which later deeply influenced *rujia* thought and thus Chinese Jewish theology, was written a century later. The second chapter of this text satirizes formal logic. In the midst of this spoof, the above statements of the logicians are parodied:

> To use a finger to demonstrate that a finger is not a finger is not as good as using a non-finger to demonstrate that a finger is not a finger. To use a horse to demonstrate that a horse is not a horse is not as good as using a non-horse to demonstrate that a horse is not a horse. Sky and Earth are one finger; the myriad things are one horse. (All translations from the Chinese are the author's own)

The last sentence of the above quotation in itself is not parody, but an explicit summation of Chinese metaphysics using the terms of these logical propositions, and it is this statement that needs to be explicated in order to understand the Chinese terminology utilized by the Kaifeng Jews to express their theological understanding in literary Chinese. This metaphysic is not a matter of abstraction arising from deductive logic, such logic not surviving in Chinese philosophy, but derives from inductive logic, reasoning based on experience, particularly the null, void, or mystic experience (*wu sang wo* "losing one's self"). (For a fuller discussion of the mystic experience, see Paper 2004.)

Although Chinese culture is polytheistic, as in other polytheistic traditions, there is an understanding of unity at the basis of everything—that is, within polytheism, monism is also found. All of the statements on cosmogony to be found in a number of early Chinese texts have variations on the same theme, which can be summed up as follows:

From Nothingness (*wu*) there arises a Somethingness (*yu*), which is nameless, so we arbitrarily name it the "Dao." The Dao, which is a oneness, divides into two. From the standpoint of energy, the two are Yin and Yang, and from the standpoint of matter are Sky and Earth (*tiandi*). In conjoining, the two produce the myriad things. Thus, Sky and Earth are the parents of all, which receive their life-force (*qi*) from the interplay of Yin and Yang.

This cosmogony is not a matter of linear time; it has neither beginning nor end. As the only constant is understood to be change, everything is in constant flux: creation is continuous and ongoing. This is called *ziran* (literally: "self thusly"), which can be translated as "nature" but also means "spontaneous creation." Everything continuously produces itself.

The primary term for Union/Unity/Oneness/Singularity/etc. is the Dao. But others terms include Taiyi (The Great Singularity—which came to be worshiped in the popular mind as a deity), Taiji (Great Ultimate—used primarily in charts and diagrams of reality), and Datung (Great Unity—which took on political meaning). A connected concept which will be relevant in the following discussion is the placing of humans into a vertical triplet: "Sky, humans and Earth"—that is, people literally exist between their equal cosmic parents, Sky and Earth, which together also represent oneness, being the initial splitting of the singular Dao.

Background II: Early Medieval Jewish theology

The Kaifeng Jews probably left Persia from the port of Basra sometime in the late tenth century. The most important Jewish thinker in that area at the time was Saadia Gaon (Saadia ben Joseph). He was born in Egypt in 882 and died in Baghdad in 942, where he had been the chief rabbi of one of the two rabbinic academies there. He is thought to have created the first *siddur* (daily prayer book) and wrote a number of treatises, including a major one on theology, *Kitab al-'Amanat wal l'tikadat (The Book of Beliefs and Opinions)*. This influential book was written in Arabic and reflected the classical Greek learning of Arab scholars, and it explicitly countered Christian theology. The Jews who arrived in China from Southwest Asia were probably aware of his thinking.

Similar to Chinese cosmogony with regard to creation beginning with nothingness (*creatio ex nihilo*), Saadia writes, "I say that our Lord, exalted be He, made it known to us that all things were created and that He had created them out of nothing" (Saadia 1948: 40). And all that is created is created out of the something that comes from the nothing (50). Because God is singular, it cannot be understood literally that humans are created in the image of God, for God being incorporeal has no image; rather, humans are "created" in the spiritual essence of God. Thus, there is a fundamental accord in these regards, although the working out differs, between the theology these Jews brought with them and the cosmogony of the educated Chinese they encountered.

Nonetheless, there are differences. For one, spontaneity of creation, as well as an ongoing creation, is specifically denied by Saadia, who writes of "the untenability of the hypothesis that a thing could create itself" (47–8). Another difference is that Saadia considered humans to be the "intended purpose of creation," and they have "been shown preference by Him above all His creatures." Thus, for Saadia, contrary to Chinese philosophy, humans are above nature (181).

The Kaifeng Jews' understanding of God

Chinese terms chosen to represent Hebrew terms for God

Several large stelae that were on the synagogue grounds and numerous plaques that decorated the Kaifeng synagogue in the Chinese fashion provide an insight into their theology. The few plaques in Hebrew are typical of those to be found in synagogues anywhere in the world even today, but the plaques in literary Chinese are unique within Judaism. Two terms—Dao and Tian in the compound *tiandi* (Sky-Earth) or alone standing for the compound—are most commonly used to refer to God. They are not direct translations of the Hebrew names to be found in the Torah but terms common to early Chinese texts as discussed above. According to the Jesuits, these terms were not simply for decorative purposes on the calligraphic plaques as they were also used by the Chinese Jews when discussing their theology with the Jesuits in the Chinese language.

Examples of this literary use of "Dao" include, "Dao is external to both somethingness and nothingness," "Dao existed prior to form [*tiandi*] and energy [*yin-yang*]," and "In understanding the Dao to be the controller of Sky, Earth and humans, we do not conceive of name or appearance." (*Daodejing* 1: "That which can be named is not the eternal name.") These theological statements which are also versions of Chinese metaphysical statements are countered in one inscription which partially reverses the relationship between Dao and Sky from a Jewish perspective: "The Dao has its origin in Sky; the fifty-three weekly portions [of the Torah—Mizrahi count] records the principles of the creation of Sky, the creation of Earth and the creation of humans."

The Chinese Jews found no serious contradiction between the Torah and the understandings expressed in Chinese. The essential prayer utterance, the Sh'ma ("Listen Israel: YHVH is our God; YHVH is singular" [Deut. 6:14]), could be understood as reiterating the essential oneness of the cosmos without being in contradiction to the Jewish theology they brought to China. YHVH being singular is equivalent to the Dao. As God, the Dao is at the beginning of all that exists. It is the state of primordial existence before differentiation takes place. Spontaneously arising out of nothingness, the Dao differentiates into Sky and Earth. In Judaism, God creates the sky and the earth from nothingness; hence, the Chinese read in this regard does take "In the beginning" (Genesis) in a direction but moderately different from the Jewish theology brought by the Jews to Kaifeng.

The major difference lies in utter non-anthropomorphism. The Dao does not create, for the Dao simply is. It is the self-division of the Dao itself that brings forth Sky and Earth, and it is Sky and Earth, as a male-female equal generative couple that spontaneously creates. And this creation is not at the beginning of time; it is ever ongoing. As Dao, God is not the primal cause of existence as expressed by Saadia, influenced by Greek philosophy revived in the Islamic universities; God is existence in and of itself.

This understanding of God is in accord with the Torah. In the Exodus story, when Moses encounters an eternal light, expressed by the metaphor of an ever-burning bush, he understands that he is in the presence of the sacred, the God of the mythic founding ancestors. The experience of merging and losing one's self in an all-encompassing intensely bright light is at the heart of the mystic experience in all traditions, as well as most near-death experiences. Moses asks God's name. God answers, "I am Existing/Existence," and further, "Thus shall you say to the children of Israel, Existence has sent me to you" (Exodus 3:1-14).

In other words, God can be understood as a Nothingness that is the source of our ancestors and is infinitely continuing existential potential (*Ein Soph* in Jewish mysticism); God is our own existence and of those we love, indeed, all of existence at all times—what is, has been and will be. God is the breathing of our lungs and the blood coursing through our arteries. If we love ever-changing life, then we love God. This interpretation is precisely in accord with a modern Haredi Jewish theologian, Tzvi Freeman (2016): "Existence itself. The flow. The infinite flow of light and energy. Of being, of existence. Of is—that is G-d." The eminent contemporary Jewish theologian, Michael Fishbane (2008: 34), writes of God as "the ultimate Source of all things . . . Life of all life."

Another Chinese understanding of Sky also accords with the Jewish understanding of YHVH. As in many cultures, in China the motion of the stars and planets are considered one of the prime indicators of the pattern of change, of the way the cosmos is naturally unfolding. Since it behooves humans to act in accordance with the way the cosmos is flowing, it is best to model one's actions or make one's choices as Sky indicates. Thus, Sky in this sense parallels an important aspect of the Jewish notion of deity. But in this understanding, God does not cause events to occur, God but indicates how events will occur. As Tian, God does not will natural events; they happen. Human affairs are not caused by God; they are the responsibility of humans, or in medieval Jewish theology, the result of "free will."

A third notion of Sky also brings together Chinese and Jewish theology. For the early Chinese, going back at least several thousand years, Sky, with its multiple meanings, was also understood as the locus of the power of the conjoined ancestral spirits, particularly for the ruling clan. Although not exactly a parallel concept, understanding God as the God of the Patriarchs, as the numinous power at the foundation of the macro-clan of the Jews, as they understood themselves in the Chinese clan-oriented context, accords with the Chinese understanding of Sky as a power above. And so the Chinese Jews also took this sense of Sky to mean God.

A point to be made with regard to the names for God in the Chinese language inscriptions is that the term for non-cosmic, non-nature deities, *shen*, is not used even once. The Chinese literati themselves made a point of avoiding the numerous deities of importance to the rest of the population, save for the numinous ancestors and the cosmic deities (which they perceived as a single deity or arising from one deity as above). Going further, the Chinese Jews avoided normative Chinese non-family, non-clan religious practices. Near the beginning of the stele dating to 1489, we find the statement, "They [Patriarchs] made no images, did not fawn upon deities (*shen*) and ghosts (*guei:* non-family dead), and gave no credence to ecstatic functionaries [popular practices relating to mediumism]." In other words, they ignored the religious elements found in non-clan temples, although they would have no problem with the Civil Temples as those revered there are not *shen* but cultural heroes, as Ezra was for the Chinese Jews.

Even though the Chinese Jews refrained from many supplementary Chinese religious practices, they did engage in the basic practices of reverencing—not worshiping—the family and clan dead, as well as the Patriarchs, which is acceptable within traditional Jewish practices. Thus, they remained fully Chinese in religion and culture as well as fully Jewish. From a Chinese standpoint, their adherence to God with Chinese names that referenced the cosmic deities and to the founders of Judaism substituted for the subsidiary popular practices, as Buddhist practices did for Chinese lay Buddhists. Chinese Buddhists also had a set of sacred texts, the Tripitaka, and a sacred language, Sanskrit.

Cosmogony and time

With regard to the Chinese concept of *ziran*, in the 1489 stele, creation is presented as completely natural: "The four seasons follow their course and the myriad creatures are birthed. . . . Living things [literally: that which is born] give birth to themselves; that which is transformed, transforms itself." Although the complete term *ziran* is not used, its meaning is clearly present with the use of *zi* (self) alone. According to the inscription, it is this basic understanding that came to Abraham as he meditated on Tian (God), and upon realizing this profound "mystery" (*xuan*), founded Judaism.

In a plaque inscription from two centuries later, we find this understanding continued in a parallel couplet: "The eternal Lord (*zhu*, a translation from the Hebrew) produces life unceasingly / The creating-transforming Tian (God) transforms the transformations unendingly." Here we have combined the Chinese understanding of continuing self-creation, self-transformation, with a creating God. But it is a continuous ever-ongoing creation-transformation, rather than a one-time event at the beginning of time.

The relationship of humans and the divine

Humans are not God, but as created from the differentiating singular Dao, humans are of the essence of God, a concept at the heart of Hellenistic Gnosticism and Jewish mysticism. As with the theology of Saadia Gaon, humans are not actually created in the image of God, for both God and the Dao have neither form nor substance and are utterly non-anthropomorphic, but in the reality of God. Humans are a manifestation of primordial existence, of existential potentiality.

But different from Saadia's theology, humans are no different from everything else that is created from the differentiation of the Dao. Humans do not have a divine mandate to rule nature. Rather, as but one manifestation of nature, they are a part of nature. Humans were given agriculture by a mythic sage emperor (culture-hero), just as they were taught to build dikes to control rampaging rivers when the snows melt or the monsoon rains arrive, and as they were given writing to enable civilization. But humans are to utilize nature wisely, carefully following the seasons and not squandering what nature provides, or through their own negligence they will suffer famine. Such understanding has been a part of Chinese philosophy at least since the time of Mengzi (Mencius, fourth century BCE).

As the Dao differentiates into male Sky and female Earth, as well as female Yin and male Yang, so that the myriad creatures can be birthed, so too humans (the Chinese term meaning "humans," *ren*, has neither gender nor number) are divided into males and females. As male Sky and female Earth, and female Yin and male Yang, are not only equal but their equality is essential to creation, so too humans as males and females are equally essential to the continued creation of humans.

Basic to the Jewish understanding of being human is the particular relationship between God and Jews. The Covenant is central to normative Jewish theology. In the Torah, the Covenant made with Abraham, reinforced during the Exodus, and symbolized by male circumcision, provided the entire context for Jewish self-understanding, at least for European Judaism. In the Tanach (complete Hebrew Bible, including the histories and the prophets), Jewish history is presented as one of repeated trials and tribulations due to how well the Jewish people accorded with the terms of this contract with God, as interpreted by the prophets. But what would this mean in a benign sociocultural context, so different from the experience of Jews living in Christian and Muslim milieus?

In the 1489 inscription there is no mention of a covenant. The ancestral teacher Abraham meditating on Sky came to understand the nature of life within the concept of *ziran*. Awakening to an understanding of this profound mystery, he sought the True Teaching (Judaism) and to assist ethereal Sky. With a unified heart/mind (*xin*), Abraham served and worshipped God, establishing the foundation of the religion which has come down to the present.

In the Torah, God introduces himself not only as the god of the forefathers but the one who had taken the Chosen People out of the land of Egypt. In the Pesach (Passover) Seder (ritual meal), much is made of the plagues God set upon the Egyptians to encourage them to give the Chosen People their freedom. In Europe, there perhaps developed even greater emphasis, as the equivalent was also wished for their Christian tormentors. But in the Chinese inscriptions, we find no mention of the Exodus, of the conquest of Canaan, of the destruction of the first temple and the Babylonian captivity. (It must be noted, however, that the Chinese Jews had *Haggadahs*, ritual texts for the Passover Seder, and thus celebrated Passover.) Is this because living in China, which has no history of religious persecution per se, let alone anti-Judaism, and not suffering for being Jews for many generations, there was no feeling of bitterness about either their situation or their neighbors? In China, the Jews prospered, not for short periods of time but for many centuries, save for suffering exactly as did the non-Jews around them at times of natural disasters or political anarchy.

Instead, the inscription of 1489 follows the giving of the Torah to Moses and its transmission through Ezra with a discussion of Jewish religious practices.

These are laid out under the categories of purity, truth, ritual, and worship. Both specifically Jewish practices and the practices unique to the Chinese Jews are described.

Hence, the special relationship between God and the Jews seems to have moved from a covenant basis to one of God being the special and sole deity for the descendants of the Patriarchs. Adherence to God is not so much a matter of contract as of *xiao* (Familism). Interestingly, Saadia Gaon in his large theological treatise mentions covenant but once, and that in the context of Jeremiah rather than the Torah [167]. Perhaps covenant became theologically more important in the West with the beginning of the Crusades in the eleventh century—the first Crusade ended up by mainly killing Jews in Europe—and the continuing horrors for the Jews. Thus, the lack of emphasis on Covenant per se may have already been a part of the understanding of God that the Jews of Kaifeng brought with them from Persia.

God and human behavior

According to the inscriptions, through the generations, the True Teaching reached Moses. Like Abraham, Moses was an exceptional person, in whom benevolence (*ren*—a different logograph from "humans") and righteousness (*yi*)—the primary *rujia* virtues—and *dao* and *de*—the primary Daoist (*daojia*) values—were perfected. Moses sought the Scriptures on Sinai, fasting and meditating for forty days and nights. His spiritual endeavors reached Sky's heart/mind (metaphorically) and thus the True Scriptures (the Torah) originated. The good persons described in the Tanach bring forth a good heart/mind in people, and the wicked persons described warn us of having a dissolute volition.

The Chinese understanding of morality is far different from the more recent traditional Jewish one which emphasizes *mitzva* [doing good and carrying out the commandments] which are rewarded and sins which are punished. From the *rujia* perspective, especially from around the time the Jewish community arose in Kaifeng, humans are understood as being innately good, the viewpoint of the *Mengzi* which was added to the Classics, although a corrupt society can turn people from acting in a good way. Good behavior means acting for the benefit of social groups, beginning with family and ending with the state. Morality is based on inferiors modeling themselves on superiors. If superiors are good, then so will those under them. Hence, the goodness of Abraham and Moses, and all the other good persons described in the Bible, are paradigms for others to emulate. One is good not from fear of punishment, but because being good is being true to one's nature, which is essentially divine, while being wicked, which in the Chinese context means acting selfishly, is being perverse to human nature. We inherently seek to be good, for which we need models to understand proper behavior. In that being good is being true to nature, it is godly.

Thus the forefathers—Abraham, Isaac, and Jacob—are the ancestors of the Jews to be ritually respected due of Familism, the core Chinese ethical value, and other transmitters of Judaism, such as Moses and Ezra, are also to be ritually respected as founders of Judaism. In the latter aspect, their treatment is similar to that of Kongzi (Confucius), Mengzi (Mencius), and so on in the *rujia* tradition.

Theodicy a nonissue

Not focusing on Covenant but understanding YHWH as existence in and of itself rather than the cause of all that happens to the Jews, meant that the nemesis of Judaism in Europe, theodicy, was not a concern. Theodicy is the quandary resulting from understanding God to be omniscient and omnipotent in juxtaposition to terrible things happening to oneself, one's family, and one's people, as well as the world as a whole. Theodicy is found throughout the Tanach—one only needs to read Job—but it became of even greater concern in Europe. Following centuries of massacres, expulsions, and pogroms, the Holocaust, when understood as God's punishment, led many Jews to become agnostics if not atheists and others to retreat into a self-imposed withdrawal from the societies and cultures around them in order to avoid the possibility of further angering God.

For the Chinese Jews, little if anything that negatively happened could be understood as a specific punishment for the Chosen People not conforming to the will of God. God is worshipped not out of fear of God but entirely out of love; this is because YHWH is perceived as the special deity of the Chinese Jews, just as Chinese Buddhists have the Buddha (who in Chinese Buddhism functions as a deity) and the Daoists have the Jade Emperor at the top of their respective pantheons. YHWH has been the God of the Jews since the time of their forefathers in the distant past, and the traditions should not only be maintained out of filial duty to one's ancestors, but because it is beautiful to do so.

> And you shall love the Lord your God with all your heart, with all your soul, and with all your might. (Deut. 6.5)

Thus God is loved for a number of reasons. As YHVH, God is loved for being the essence of existence, and existence for the Jews in China on the whole was very good. God is also loved as the patron deity of the Jews. As Sky, God is loved in being the sum total of all the prior spirits of the Jews who existed in the past, of the chain of being from Abraham to the present as exemplified in the tradition, as well as for the tradition in and of itself. God is loved as the pattern of events, of all that happens. But God being non-anthropomorphic, what happens is understood as unwilled and not involving human emotions such as jealousy and anger, or human actions such as punishment. (In Western texts, the Chinese concept of the "Mandate of Heaven [Sky]" tends to be interpreted from a Judeo-Christian standpoint as the "Will of Heaven," rather than the Chinese meaning of "Sky Pattern.")

God and Torah

For Saadia Gaon as discussed above, as well as for Maimonides a century later, and for the Chinese Jews, God is not simply non-anthropomorphic; rather, God is formless and equivalent to nothingness. This understanding of God is equally found in Christian and Islamic mysticism, and continues in Jewish mysticism. With the emergence of the Kabalistic tradition in the thirteenth century, the term for the ultimate, for God as an undifferentiated unity, as the Nothingness with which one merges in the mystic experience, is '*Eiyn Sof*, the Infinite.

Thus, the question might arise as to how for the Chinese Jews this accorded with their reverence and love for the Torah, replete with frequent depictions of a highly anthropomorphic God. A simple answer would be that they dealt with it no different than Saadia Gaon and Maimonides, as well as Jewish mystics throughout the ages: they did not see it as a problem. In part, this is because God is not the functional center of Judaism; it is the Torah. Even today in North America, for the many Jews who are agnostic if not atheistic due to the Holocaust, the Torah itself remains sacred.

For the Chinese Jews, the Torah was sacred, not because it was the word of God, since God has no mouth from which to speak, but because it has been the very heart of Judaism since it began. It is the text which is reverenced, as is the Classics for the *rujia* tradition, the Tripitaka for the Buddhist tradition, and the Canon for the Daoist tradition. All of these texts are semi-sacred because of their central historical significance. They are also semi-sacred simply because they are written, which in itself is sacred, even more so in China than in traditional Judaism, as writing in China is the primary means for communication with the numinous, a practice which goes back to the proto-historic period and the inception of writing. They are further semi-sacred in the Jewish and Chinese

Buddhist traditions, because the rituals focus on them. All of these texts are understood to require interpretation and have extensive commentaries. Hence, the anthropomorphism of the Torah would have been perceived as symbolic, as metaphor, and so on, and not to be understood literally.

Conclusion

In summary, for the Chinese Jews, God is the formless numinous power which continuously gives rise to life and to which life is beholden for its very existence. God is loved beyond one's mother and father, because God is the ultimate parent, not only for each individual, but for the Jewish people, a macro-clan, as a whole. Hence, God fits into the pattern of Familism in China. (A more complete exposition of the above as well as corollary material and discussion will be found in Paper 2012.) While Neo-Confucian thinking and terminology harmoniously melded with the theology brought from Baghdad creating a relatively new theological synthesis, the Chinese Jews maintained the normative ("Orthodox") Jewish life of prayer, study, festivals, *kashrut*, and other practices (see Simons 2010). Therefore, Chinese Judaism was fully Jewish with a Chinese flavor—perhaps, if one were being flippant, one could say that it was similar to kosher Chinese cuisine.

Epilogue: Chinese Religion Today in China and the Chinese Diaspora

The religions of humans, if viewed from a global perspective, are not as diverse as usually presumed. Given that we *Homo sapiens* evolved over two hundred thousand years ago, humans lived a gathering-hunting lifestyle for most of this time, and religion everywhere followed a similar general pattern integral to foraging cultures. Beginning around fourteen thousand to twelve thousand years ago, some humans began to live in settlements in those coastal areas with a rich year-round maritime environment, as along the coasts of present-day Northwest North America and northern Chile. This was followed around ten thousand years ago with settled horticulture around the temperate and subtropical parts of the world, where there was sufficient water and sunlight. Settlement led to Familism as delineated in Chapter 2 and as documented in Chapter 1 with regard to China.

Horticulture evolved into agriculture, which led to class distinctions, the earliest social class being professional warriors, which eventually led to kingdoms and then to empires. This pattern can be found around the globe, and its continuity is documented in Chinese civilization. Familism continued in the agricultural setting and in the industrial milieu which followed and continues in the contemporary electronic culture. Once Familism evolved, it seems to have flourished except where religions of individual salvation developed unmodified by Familism, as in the Christian West.

Although China borrowed Marxist-Leninist communism based on an industrial proletariat, Mao and his colleagues modified it to fit an agrarian peasantry and imbued it with humane aspects of Familism, although this was temporarily lost with the Great Leap Forward, in an attempt to industrialize in spite of the American embargo, and with the Cultural Revolution, brought on by the frustration engendered by the embargo. Since that time, China has moved away from Western influence and reinvigorated Chinese Religion, in spite of continued American attempts to place it under American Christian influence, which is presently being countered. Familism is now explicitly promoted in China as the basis of Chinese civilization. Thus, Familism continues unabated in contemporary China, as well as Korea (including Korean indigenous Christianity: the Unification Church) and Japan.

Due to a large expanding population until the government brought it under control with the temporary one-child policy, from the second half of the nineteenth century through the early twentieth, millions of Chinese left the southeastern coastal area to work in the gold mines and build the transcontinental railroads of North America, to work as laborers in Europe during the First World War, to create small and large businesses throughout Southeast Asia, Indonesia and the Pacific Islands, and more recently from all over China for education and business opportunities around the world. This has led to Chinese diaspora communities in many places.

In the diaspora communities, Chinese Religion continues among many with little if any change. This can be seen by going into stores serving the larger diaspora communities, such as Toronto, Vancouver, and Victoria, with which I am familiar. There one will find incense and spirit money for offerings, paper clothing and other necessities to be burned for use by the dead, small shrines and images of deities, the cups and other paraphernalia used on altars, and red metal containers on wheels for burning offerings. At the time of the Spring Festival, these stores carry appropriate red decorations to celebrate the New Year. In other words, Chinese Religion is not only alive and well in China but also can be found wherever diaspora Chinese communities are found.

Appendix: Chronological Chart

Shang Dynasty	? −1100 +/−50 BCE
Zhou Dynasty	to 255 BCE
Qin Dynasty	221–207 BCE
Han Dynasty	206 BCE–CE 220
Sui Dynasty	589–618
Tang Dynasty	618–905
Northern Song Dynasty	960–1126
Southern Song Dynasty	1127–1278
Yuan (Mongol) Dynasty	1280–1368
Ming Dynasty	1368–1644
Qing (Manchu) Dynasty	1644–1911

References

Adler, Joseph A. 2002. *Chinese Religious Traditions*. London: Pearson.

Bays, Daniel H. 2012. *A New History of Christianity in China*. West Sussex: Wiley-Blackwell.

Bering, Jesse M. and D. D. P. Johnson. 2005. "'O Lord ... You Perceive My Thoughts from Afar': Recursiveness and the Evolution of Supernatural Agency." *Journal of Cognition and Culture* 5: 118–42.

Bering, Jesse M. and D. D. P. Johnson. 2006. "Hand in God, Mind of Man: Punishment and Cognition in the Evolution of Cooperation." *Evolutionary Psychology* 4: 219–33.

Bloch, Maurice. 2010. "Is There Religion at Çatalhöyük ... or Are There Just Houses?" In *Religions in the Emergence of Civilization: Çatalhöyük as a Case Study*. Edited by Ian Hodder: 146–62.

Blum, Jason N. 2018. "Belief: Problems and Pseudo-Problems." *Journal of the American Academy of Religion* 86/3: 642–64.

Boethius. 2004. *On the Holy Trinity (De Trinitate)*. Translated by Erik C. Kenyon. http://pvspade.com/Logic/docs/BoethiusDeTrin.pdf (accessed November 27, 2015).

Bush, Susan. 1971. *The Chinese Literati on Painting, Su Shi (1037–1101) to Tung Ch'i-ch'ang (1555–1636)*. Cambridge: Harvard University Press.

Cahill, Suzanne. 1993. *Transcendence and Divine Passion: The Queen Mother of the West in Medieval China*. Stanford: Stanford University Press.

Chang, Chu-Kuen. 1977. "Korean Folk Belief: Shamanism and Shaman-Song in Cheju Island." In *Korean and Asian Religious Tradition*. Edited by Chai-Shin Yu. Toronto: Korean and Related Studies Press.

Chen Shuguo. 2010. "State Religious Ceremonials." Translated by Keith Knapp. In John Lagerwey and Lü Pengzhi. *Early Chinese Religion, Part Two: The Period of Division (220–589 AD)*. 2 vols. Leiden: Brill: vol. 1. 53–142.

Chen Yinko [Chen Yin'ge]. 1932. "Tianshidao yu binhai diyu zhi guanxi." *Bulletin of the National Research Institute of History and Philosophy*. Taipei: Academia Sinica.

Cheng, Manchao. 1995. *The Origin of Chinese Deities*. Beijing: Foreign Languages Press.

Ch'ü, T'ungtsu. 1962. *Local Government in China under the Ch'ing*. Cambridge: Harvard University Press.

Clark, James Kelly and Justin T. Winslett. 2011. "The Evolutionary Psychology of Chinese Religion: Pre-Qin High Gods and Punishers and Rewarders." *Journal of the American Academy of Religion* 79: 928–60.

Clark, James Kelly and Justin T. Winslett. 2012. "Rejoinder." *Journal of the American Academy of Religion* 80: 522–24.

Clart, Philip. 2003. "Moral Mediums: Spirit-Writing and the Cultural Construction of Chinese Spirit-Mediumship." *Ethnologies* 25: 153–90.

Clart, Philip and Paul Crowe. eds. 2009. *The People and the Dao: New Studies in Chinese Religions in Honour of Daniel L. Overmyer*. Monumenta Serica Monograph Series LX.

Conboy, Kenneth and James Morrison. 2002. *The CIA's Secret War in Tibet*. Lawrence: University Press of Kansas.

Confucius. 1979. *The Analects (Lun yü)*. Translated by D. C. Lau. Harmondsworth: Penguin Books.

Confucius. 1998. *The Analects of Confucius: A Philosophical Translation*. Translated by Roger T. Ames and Henry Rosemont, Jr. New York: Ballantine Books.

Confucius. 2003. *Analects: With Selections from Traditional Commentaries*. Translated by Edward Slingerland. Indianapolis: Hackett Publishing Company.

Creel, H. G. 1932. "Was Confucius Agnostic?" *T'oung Pao* 29: 55–99.

Creel, H. G. 1949. *Confucius and the Chinese Way*. New York: Harper & Row.

d'Aguili, Eugene G. and Andrew B. Newberg. 1999. *The Mystical Mind: Probing the Biology of Religious Experience*. Minneapolis: Fortress Press.

Davis, Edward L. 2001. *Society and the Supernatural in Song China*. Honolulu: University of Hawaii Press.

Dean, Kenneth. 1993. *Taoist Ritual and Popular Cults of Southeast China*. Princeton: Princeton University Press.

de Groot, J. J. M. 1894. *The Religious System of China*: vol. 6. Leyden: E.J. Brill.

Dowell, William. May 10, 1999. "Interview with Li Hongzhi." *Time* (online).

Drinnon, Richard. 1980. *Facing West: The Metaphysics of Indian-Hating and Empire-Building*. New York: New American Library.

Dubuisson, Daniel. 2003. *The Western Construction of Religion: Myths, Knowledge, and Ideology*. Translated by William Sayers. Baltimore: John Hopkins University Press.

Ebrey, Patricia Buckley. 1991. *Chu Hsi's Family Rituals*. Princeton: Princeton University Press.

Eliade, Mircea. 1964. *Shamanism: Archaic Techniques of Ecstasy*. Translated by Willard R. Trask. Princeton: Princeton University Press.

Encyclopædia Britannica. 2015. http://www.britannica.com/topic/High-God (accessed November 30, 2015).

Eno, Robert. 1990a. *The Confucian Creation of Heaven*. Albany: State University of New York Press.

Eno, Robert. 1990b. "Was There a High God Ti in Shang Religion." *Early China* 15: 1–26.

Eno, Robert. 2007. "Shang State Religion and the Pantheon of the Oracle Texts." In *Early Chinese Religion, Part One: Shang through Han (1250 BC-220 AD)*. Edited by John Lagerwey and Marc Kalinowski. Leiden: Brill: vol. I. 41–102.

Evans, G. R. 1980. *Old Arts and New Theology: The Beginnings of Theology as an Academic Discipline*. Oxford: Clarendon Press.

"Falun Gong Jams Official Chinese TV." July 09, 2002. *The Washington Post*.

Feuchtwang, Stephan. 1978. "School Temple and City God." In *Studies in Chinese Society*. Edited by Arthur P. Wolf. Stanford: Stanford University Press: 103–30.

Fishbane, Michael. 2008. *Sacred Attunement: A Jewish Theology*. Chicago: University of Chicago Press.

Focus Taiwan news channel. 2018-12-23 19:49:13 & 2019-01-07 20:06:37. http://focustai wan.tw/views/page/search/hysearchws.aspx?q=city%20god%20temple (accessed January 13, 2019).

Fong, Wen. 1976. "Archaism as a 'Primitive' Style." In *Artist and Traditions*. Edited by Christian F. Murck. Princeton: Princeton University Press.

Fowler, Jeaneane and Merv Fowler. 2008. *Chinese Religion*. Sussex Academic Press.

Freeman, Tzvi. http://www.chabad.org/libary/article_cdo/aid/1595892/jewish/What-is-Gd.htm (accessed May, 2019).

Frontline. 1995. "The Gate of Heavenly Peace." http://www.pbs.org./wgbh/pages/fron tline/pograms/info/1418.html

Gernet, Jacques. 1956. *Les Aspects économiques du bouddhisme dans la société chinoise du Ve au Xe siècle*. Publications de l'École française d'Extréme-Orient, 39. École française d'Extrême-Orient (Paris: Impr. nationale): Saigon.

Gernet, Jacques. 1985. *China and the Christian Impact*. Translated by J. Lloyd. Cambridge: Cambridge University Press.

Girardot, Norman. 1992. "Very Small Books about Large Subjects: A Prefatory Appreciation of the Enduring Legacy of Laurence G. Thompson's Chinese Religion, An Introduction." *Journal of Chinese Religions* 20: 9–15.

Gordon, Richard and Carmen Hinton. 1995. *The Gate of Heavenly Peace* [documentary film]. Brookline: Long Bow Group.

Graham, A. C. 1960. *The Book of Lieh-tzŭ*. London: John Murray.

Grimshaw, Anna. 1992. *Servants of the Buddha: Winter in a Himalayan Convent*. London: Open Letters – reprinted by Cleveland: The Pilgrim Press, 1994.

Guthrie, Elliot. 2014. "Religion as Anthropomorphism at Çatalhöyük." In *Religion at Work in a Neolithic Society: Vital Matters*. Edited by Ian Hodder. Cambridge: Cambridge University Press: 86–108.

Hansen, Chad. 1993. "Chinese Ideographs and Western Ideas." *Journal of Asian Studies* 52: 373–99.

Hansen, Valerie. 1990. *Changing Gods in Medieval China, 1127–1276*. Princeton: Princeton University Press.

Hodder, Ian. ed. 2010. *Religions in the Emergence of Civilization: Çatalhöyük as a Case Study*. Cambridge: Cambridge University Press.

Hodder, Ian. ed. 2014a. *Religion at Work in a Neolithic Society: Vital Matters*. Cambridge: Cambridge University Press.

Hodder, Ian. 2014b. "The Vitalities of Çatalhöyük." In *Religion at Work in a Neolithic Society: Vital Matters*. Edited by Ian Hodder. Cambridge: Cambridge University Press: 1–32.

Hu, Anning and Felicia F. Tian. 2018. "Still under the Ancestors' Shadow? Ancestor Worship and Family Formation in Contemporary China." *Demographic Research*. http://www.demographic-research.org/Volumes/Vol38/1/DOI: 10.4054/DemRes.2018.38.1

Huang, Liu Hung. 1984. *A Complete Book of Happiness and Benevolence (Fuhui ch'üan-shu), A Manual for Local Magistrates in Seventeenth-Century China*. Translated by Lang Chu. Tucson: University of Arizona Press.

Huang, Yong. 2007. "Confucian Theology: Three Models." *Religion Compass* 1: 455–78.

Hugar, Wayne R. 2016. "*Surprise!* What Caused China's Recent and Massive Land Reclamation in the South China Sea?" *Journal of Strategic Intelligence* Summer: 4–36.

Jordan, David K. 1972. *Gods, Ghosts, and Ancestors: Folk Religion in a Taiwanese Village*. Berkeley: University of California Press.

Jordan, David K. and Daniel L. Overmyer. 1986. *The Flying Phoenix: Aspects of Chinese Sectarianism in Taiwan*. Princeton: Princeton University Press.

Karkgren, Berhnard. 1950. *The Book of Odes*. Stockholm: Museum of Far Eastern Antiquities.

Ke, Yuan. 1993. *Dragons and Dynasties: An Introduction to Chinese Mythology*. Translated by Kin Echlin and Nie Zhixiong. New York: Penguin Books.

Keightly, David. 1978. "The Religious Commitment: Shang Theology and the Genesis of Chinese Political Culture." *History of Religions* 17: 211–25.

Kessell, John L. 1978. "Diego Romero, the Plains Apaches, and the Inquisition." *The American West* 15/3: 12–16.

Kitagawa, Joseph. 1991. "Dimensions of the East Asian Religious Universe." *History of Religions* 31/2: 181–209.

Lai, David. 2011. *The United States and China in Power Transition*. Carlisle: U.S. War College, Strategic Studies Institute Book.

Lai, David Chuenyan, Jordan Paper, and Li Chuang Paper. 2005. "The Chinese in Canada: Their Unrecognized Religion." In *Religion and Ethnicity in Canada*. Edited by Paul Bramadat and David Seljak. Toronto: Pearson Longman.

Lai, Zongxian. 1999. *Taiwan Daojiao yuanliu* [The origin and development of Daoism in Taiwan]. Taipei: Zhonghua daotong.

Lagerway, John. 1987. *Taoist Ritual in Chinese Society and History*. New York: MacMillan Publishing Co.

Lagerway, John and Marc Kalinowski. eds. 2007. *Early Chinese Religion, Part One: Shang through Han*: vol. 2. Leiden: Brill.

Lamb, F. Bruce. 1974. *Wizard of the Upper Amazon: The Story of Manuel Córdova-Rios*. Berkeley: North Atlantic Books.

Latourette, Kenneth Scott. 1929. *A History of the Christian Missions in China*. New York: MacMillan.

Lau, D. C. 1963. *Lao Tzu: Tao Te Ching*. Harmondsworth: Penguin Books.

Laytner, Anson H. and Jordan Paper. eds. 2017. *The Chinese Jews of Kiafeng: A Millennium of Adaptation and Endurance*. Lanham: Lexington Books.

Ledderose, Lothar. 1977. "Some Taoist Elements in Six Dynasties Calligraphy" New Haven: Paper Presented at the Yale University Conference on Chinese Calligraphy.

Ledderose, Lothar. 1979. *Mi Fu and the Classical Tradition of Chinese Calligraphy*. Princeton: Princeton University Press.

Leslie, Donald Daniel. 1972. *The Survival of the Chinese Jews: The Jewish Community of Kaifeng*. Leiden: E. J. Brill.

Lewis, I. M. 1971. *Ecstatic Religion: An Anthropological Study of Spirit Possession and Shamanism*. Harmondsworth: Penguin Books.

Lin, Yutang. 1947. *The Gay Genius*. New York: John Day.

Louden, Robert B. 2002. "'What Does Heaven Say?' Christian Wolff and Western Interpretations of Confucian Ethics." In *Confucius and the Analects: New Essays*. Edited by Bryan W. van Norden. Oxford: Oxford University Press: 73–93.

Machle, Edward J. 1993. *Nature and Heaven in the Xunzi: A Study of the Tian Lun*. Albany: State University of New York Press.

Mattis, General Jim. 2018. *Jim Mattis's Resignation Letter to Donald Trump*. www.theguardian.com/us-news/2018/dec/21/jim-mattis-resigns-as-defense-secretary-letter-in-full

McDermott, Gerald R. 2011. *World Religions*. Nashville: Thomas Nelson.

Mencken, H. L. July 26, 1920. "Bayard vs. Lionheart." *The Evening Sun (Baltimore Evening Sun)*. Baltimore: Tribune Publishing: Page 8, Column 5.

Meyer, Jeffrey F. 1991. *The Dragons of Tiananmen: Beijing as a Sacred City*. Columbia: University of South Carolina Press.

Nakamura, Hajime. 1964. *Ways of Thinking of Eastern Peoples*. Translated by Philip P. Wiener. Honolulu: East-West Center Press.

Nylan, Michael and Thomas Wilson. 2010. *Lives of Confucius: Civilization's Greatest Sage through the Ages*. New York: Doubleday.

Overmyer, Daniel. 1989. "Attitudes Towards Popular Religion in Ritual Texts of the Chinese State: The Collected Statutes of the Great Ming." *Cahiers d'Extréme-Asie* 5: 191–221.

Overmyer, Daniel. 2002."Comments on the Foundations of Chinese Culture in Late Traditional Times." In *Ethnography in China Today: A Critical Assessment of Methods and Results*. Edited by Daniel L. Overmyer. Taipei: Yuan-Liou Publishing Co.

Pan, Dawei. 2017. "Is Chinese Culture Dualist? An Answer to Edward Slingerland from a Medical Philosophical Viewpoint." *Journal of the American Academy of Religion* 4: 1016–31.

Paper, Jordan. 1983. "The Post-Contact Origin of an American Indian High God: The Suppression of Feminine Spirituality." *American Indian Quarterly* 7/4: 1–24.

Paper, Jordan. 1986. "The Divine Principle: The Bible from a Korean Perspective." *Studies in Religion* 15/4: 451–60.

Paper, Jordan. 1987. *The Fu-Tzu: A Post-Han Confucian Text*. Leiden: E.J. Brill (*T'oung Pao* Monograph XIII).

Paper, Jordan. 1989. "The Normative East Asian Understanding of Christian Scriptures." *Studies in Religion* 18/4: 451–65.

Paper, Jordan. 1991. "Religious Studies: Time to Move from a Eurocentric Bias?" In *Religious Studies: Issues, Prospects and Proposals*. Edited By Klous K. Klostermaier and Larry W. Hurtado. Atlanta: Scholars Press: 73–84.

Paper, Jordan. 1993. Religious Transformations and Socio-Political Change: A Western Eurocentric Paradigm? In *Religious Transformations and Socio-Political Change: Eastern Europe and Latin America*. Edited by L. H. Martin. Berlin: Walter de Gruyter: 61–72.

Paper, Jordan. 1995a. "Foreign Religions and Chinese Culture: Comparative Paradigms." In *Religion and Modernization in China: Proceedings of the Regional Conference of the International Association for the History of Religions, Beijing, China, April 1992*. Edited by Dai Kangsheng, Zhang Yinying, and Michael Pye. Cambridge: Roots and Branches: 167–78.

Paper, Jordan. 1995b. *"The Spirits Are Drunk": Comparative Approaches to Chinese Religion*. Albany: State University of New York Press.

Paper, Jordan. 1996a. "Mediums and Modernity: The Institutionalization of Ecstatic Religious Functionaries in Taiwan." *Journal of Chinese Religions* 24: 105–29.

Paper, Jordan. 1996b. "Religions in Contact: The Effects of Domination from a Comparative Perspective." In *Religions in Contact: Selected Proceedings of the Special IAHR Conference, Brno, August 1994*. Edited by Iva Dolealová, Betislav Horyna, and Dalibor Papoušek. Brno: Czech Society for the Study of Religion: 39–56.

Paper, Jordan. 1997. *Through the Earth Darkly: Female Spirituality in Comparative Perspective*. New York: Continuum.

Paper, Jordan. 2004. *The Mystic Experience: A Descriptive and Comparative Analysis*. Albany: State University of New York Press.

Paper, Jordan. 2005. *The Deities are Many: A Polytheistic Theology*. Albany: State University of New York Press.

Paper, Jordan. 2007. *Native North American Religious Traditions: Dancing for Life*. Westport: Praeger.

Paper, Jordan. 2009. "The Role of Possession Trance in Chinese Culture and Religion: A Comparative Overview from the Neolithic to the Present." In *The People and the Dao: New Studies in Chinese Religions in Honour of Daniel L. Overmyer*. Edited by Philip Clart and Paul Crowe. Monumenta Serica Monograph Series LX: 327–45.

Paper, Jordan. 2012a. *The Theology of the Chinese Jews, 1000–1850*. Waterloo: Wilfrid Laurier University Press.

Paper, Jordan. 2012b. "Response to Kelly James Clark and Justin T. Winslett, 'The Evolutionary Psychology of Chinese Religion: Pre-Qin High Gods as Punishers and Rewarders' 79/4: 928–960." *Journal of the American Academy of Religion* 80/2: 518–21.

Paper, Jordan. 2013. "A New Approach to Understanding Chinese Religion." *Huaren zongjiao yenjio* [Studies in Chinese Religion] 1: 1–33.

Paper, Jordan. 2016. *Through the Earth Darkly: Female Spirituality in Comparative Perspective*. London: Bloomsbury (Continuum 1999).

Paper, Jordan. 2017. "The Issue of the Jewishness of the Chinese Jewish Magistrates." In *The Chinese Jews of Kiafeng: A Millennium of Adaptation and Endurance*. Edited by Anson H. Laytner and Jordan Paper. Lanham: Lexington Books: 83–95.

Paul Radin 1923. "The Winnebago Tribe," *Bureau of American Ethnology, Smithsonian Institution, 37th Annual Report*: 1–511.

People's Daily. March 25, 2016. "Xiao Is the Basis of Virtue" [translated from Chinese].

Poceski, Mario. 2009. *Introducing Chinese Religion.* London: Routledge.

Pukai, Mary Kawena et al. 1972. *Nānā I Ke Kumu (Look to the Source)*: vol. I. Honolulu: Hui Hānai.

Qingdai qiju zhuce (Daily Life Register of the Qing Dynasty) – this extract, couched in modern Chinese, has been circulating on the internet without reference to its specific location within the multi-volume work.

Reischauer, Edwin O. 1955. *Ennin's Diary: The Record of a Pilgrimage to China in Search of the Law.* New York: Ronald.

Ricci, Matteo. 1953. *China in the Sixteenth Century: The Journals of Matthew Ricci: 1583–1610.* Translated by Louis J. Gallagher. New York: Random House.

Rosemont, Henry Jr. and Roger T. Ames. 2009. *The Chinese Classic of Family Reverence.* Honolulu: University of Hawaii Press.

Roth, Harold D. 2008. "Against Cognitive Imperialism: A Call for a Non-Ethnocentric Approach to Cognitive Science and Religious Studies." *Religion East & West* 8/ October: 1–26.

Saadia Gaon. 1948. *The Book of Beliefs and Opinions.* Translated by Samuel Rosenblatt. New Haven: Yale University Press.

Saso, Michael R. 1972. *Taoism and the Rite of Cosmic Renewal.* Pullman, WA: Washington State University Press.

Saso, Michael R. 1978. *The Teachings of Taoist Master Chuang.* New Haven: Yale University Press.

Saso, Michael R. 1990. *Blue Dragon White Tiger: Taoist Rites of Passage.* Washington, DC: The Daoist Center.

Schilbrack, Kevin. 2014. *Philosophy and the Study of Religion: A Manifesto.* Malden: Wiley Blackwell.

Schipper, Kristopher. 1993 (1982). *The Daoist Body.* Translated by Karen C. Duval. Berkeley: University of California Press.

Shahar, Meir. 1998. *Crazy Ji: Chinese Religion and Popular Literature.* Cambridge: Harvard University Asia Center.

Shultes, F. LeRon. 2014. "Excavating Theogonies: Anthropomorphic Promiscuity and Sociographic Prudery in the Neolithic and Now." In *Religion at Work in a Neolithic Society: Vital Matters.* Edited by Ian Hodder. Cambridge: Cambridge University Press: 58–85.

Simons, Rabbi Dr. Chaim. 2010. *Jewish Religious Observance by the Jews of Kaifeng China*: vol. 5. Seattle: Sino-Judaic Institute, Sinojudaica Series.

Soothill, W. E. 1913. *The Three Religions of China.* London: Hodder & Staughton.

(Staff). (Guidebook to) *The Museum of Anatolian Civilizations.* Ankara: no date— purchased at the museum in 1999.

State Department. 1989. http://www.gwu.edu/~nsarchiv/NSAEBB/NSAEBB16/docum
  ents/1 & 3

Statesman (India).| November 3, 2010 [on-line]: "CPC Officials' Visit to Temple Sparks
  Off Debate over Ideology."

Szto, Mary. 2011. "Strengthening the Rule of Virtue and Finding Chinese Law in
  'Other' Places: Gods, Kin, Guilds and Gifts." http://works.bepress.com/mary_szto/3
  (accessed July 17, 2012).

Tan, L. H. et al. 2000. "Brain Activation in the Processing of Chinese Characters and
  Words: A Functional MRI Study." *Human Brain Mapping* 10: 16–27.

Tan, L. H. et al. 2001. "The Neural System Underlying Chinese Logograph Reading."
  Neuro-Image 13: 836–46.

Tang, Yiyuan et al. 2006. "Arithmetic Processing in the Brain Shaped by Cultures."
  Proceedings of the National Academy of Sciences of the United States 103: 10775–80.

Thompson, Laurence. 1989. *Chinese Religion*. 4th edn. Belmont: Wadsworth Publishing.

Trigger, Bruce G. 1976. *The Children of Aataentsic: A History of the Huron People to
  1660*. Kingston: McGill-Queen's University Press.

U.S. Government. 2017. *The United States and China in Power Transition – Chinese
  History, Uyghurs, Sun Yat-Sen, Taiwan, Spratly and Senkaku Islands, Tibet, Dalai
  Lama, Xinjiang, Han Chinese*. Progressive Management Publications.

Van Gulik, Robert Hans. 1956. *T'ang-yin-pi-shih, "Parallel Cases from under the Pear-
  tree" A 13th Century Manual of Jurisprudence and Detection*. Leiden: Brill.

Van Gulik, Robert Hans. 1958. *The Chinese Bell Murders*. New York: Harper & Row.

van Huyssteen, J. Wentzel. 2014. "The Historical Self: Memory and Religion at
  Çatalhöyük." In *Religion at Work in a Neolithic Society: Vital Matters*. Edited by Ian
  Hodder. Cambridge: Cambridge University Press: 109–33.

Watts, John R. 1972. *The District Magistrate in Late Imperial China*. New York:
  Columbia University Press.

Weiner, Tim. 2008. *Legacy of Ashes: The History of the CIA*. New York: Anchor Books.

White, William Charles. 1966. *Chinese Jews*. 2nd edn. Toronto: University of Toronto
  Press.

Yang, C. K. 1967. *Religion in Chinese Society*. Berkeley: University of California Press.

Yang, Lihui and An Deming. 2005. *Handbook of Chinese Mythology*. Oxford: Oxford
  University Press.

Yü Chün-fang. 2001. *The Chinese Transformation of Avalokitesvara*. New York:
  Columbia University Press.

Zito, A. R. 1987. "City Gods, Filiality, and Hegemony in Late Imperial China." *Modern
  China* 13: 333–71.

Index

www.ingramcontent.com/pod-product-compliance
Lightning Source LLC
Chambersburg PA
CBHW062029270326
41929CB00014B/2379